PARKINSON'S DISEASE

An Insider's Perspective to Reduce the
Symptoms Through Music Therapy

ROGER LEE

Inspiring Voices®

Inspiring Voices books may be ordered through booksellers or by contacting:

Inspiring Voices
1663 Liberty Drive
Bloomington, IN 47403
www.inspiringvoices.com
1 (866) 697-5313

Illustrations by Elise Deppe.

Scripture quotations are taken from The Authorized (King James) Version of the Bible ('the KJV'), the rights in which are vested in the Crown in the United Kingdom, is reproduced here by permission of the Crown's patentee, Cambridge University Press.

ISBN: 978-1-4624-1265-5 (sc)
ISBN: 978-1-4624-1266-2 (e)

Library of Congress Control Number: 2019904523

Print information available on the last page.

Inspiring Voices rev. date: 8/02/2019

Dedication and Acknowledgement

This book is dedicated to my brother Richard G. Lee, who battled with Parkinson's for a number of years and passed away September 18th, 2018.

PREFACE

My purpose in writing this book is not to make a huge income, but rather, to make a huge outcome. Moreover, I do not wish to foist any particular religion upon the readers of my book, but merely to suggest that a spiritual element, based on Jesus Christ, should be included in the treatment of Parkinson's Disease (PD). The recommended additional treatment is called Music Therapy and should be integrated with the three fundamental existing therapies. With the use of classical and spiritual music, as well as, Christian principles, a fourth element ought to be included as a viable complementary therapy. It would indeed create stability and coordination with all the various therapists involved, thereby establishing a comprehensive and holistic strategy in the treatment of PD. Based on my personal experience, the current PD treatments are mainly threefold:

(1)   Participate in an exercise program with a physical therapist.
(2)   Take medication as prescribed by a medical doctor.
(3)   Become a member of a local PD support group.

These treatments deal with and relate to the physical, mental, and social elements of an individual. The spiritual dimension of a person tends to be omitted. However, the service and care to which I have received are beyond reproach. In short, the medical care afforded to me has been impeccable. Therefore, I am not, in any way, being critical of the current system; rather I am merely suggesting that a spiritual music element be included, thereby making PD Therapy more complete and robust. Thus, the intent of the book is to advocate for Music Therapy (MT) in a fair amount of detail.

Included as a part of Music Therapy is Neurologic Music Therapy (NMT), the focus is the brain. For example, the adverse effect of heavy metal music on the brain is analyzed. Empirical research has revealed that adversity is another means by which individuals can enhance their creativity with the utilization of different parts of the brain. Later Chapters explain how Neurologic Music Therapy and traditional Music Therapy can assist people in coping with common PD non-motor symptoms such as depression, anxiety, stress, adversity, and excessive financial debt as a result of impulsive buying. Moreover, analysis of PET scans has shown that the cerebellum is larger in the brains of musicians than in those of non-musicians. The fine motor control skills needed to play musical instruments are encoded within a larger cerebellum. Musical knowledge learned over several years of arduous but necessary and proper practice is stored in the cerebrum which is directly connected to the cerebellum.

The basis upon which Music Therapy is implemented is listening to and playing of inspirational music. The presupposition is that Mozart's music is the standard or benchmark for spiritual music. I am not suggesting or advocating that PD patients discontinue any of their current treatments. The notion is to keep applying the treatments in the aforementioned three categories and add Spiritual Music Therapy as a fourth element. Music Therapy is usually the medium to include and enhance the spiritual aspect of PD therapy. Music Therapy is intended to be complementary and integrative in nature; it's neither mutually exclusive, nor adversarial. This 4th component or dimension would be akin to adding a 4th leg to a three-legged stool. The fourth leg would buttress, reinforce, and balance the stool and in a similar analogous way adding Music Therapy should enhance a PD patient's overall therapy. Remember the patient's' existing treatments and therapy SHOULD NEITHER BE CURTAILED, NOR MODIFIED save it be only by a medical doctor's order. The suggested fourth leg adds the spiritual dimension of healing and serves as a complementary therapy to the other therapies. Each leg would represent one of the four therapies for PD patients, and thereby deal with the patient's physical, spiritual, mental, and social elements.

One advantage of utilizing Music Therapy is that it can be implemented concurrently with the other therapies without being intrusive or distracting. Also, there are no side effects. I can attest to the fact that music is not only very therapeutic but also fun. While serving in Vietnam, I had a six string and a 12 string guitar. I had a guitar while serving a religious, two-year mission in Brazil. I used to "jam" with my friends when I was in college. I have played my banjo a few times during physical therapy sessions, and during our support group meetings. Our leader of the support group to which I belong asked me to play my banjo and after I played, he emailed me and said it was "awesome." Remember, I am not a professional musician.

Each one of the four treatments would be equal in standing with respect to emphasis and importance. This holistic methodology would not replace or preclude applying any current therapy in use. When all four therapies are used concurrently, in a collaborative manner, there is no opportunity cost, in which a patient would have to end one or more therapies, because of financial and/or time constraints, in order to apply Music Therapy. Finally, the outcome is more than the sum of each therapy's contribution. Accordingly, a synergistic effect is the outcome.

As I was contemplating the organization of my proposed book, I subsequently said to myself, "Self, who am I, trying to write a book about PD therapies?" You have not earned any academic credentials in health care. Your only exposure to health care has been minimal training while serving as a field medic in the U.S. Army, in Vietnam. You are a Nobody in health care, and nobody will read Nobody's book." But I suddenly realized that I am Somebody who has had PD for about 10 years and has gained an inordinate amount off practical experience with this repugnant disease. Indeed, I can become a Somebody by illuminating the diverse non-motor PD symptoms and therapies which tend to be treated too lightly in my judgment. Also, I have acquired a significant amount of sound experience with PD motor symptoms and therapies.

Hopefully, somebody will read Somebody's book and discuss the merits of Somebody's book with somebody. Thus, Somebody's book should make a meaningful and purposeful contribution to the body of knowledge about PD.

On a serious note, one of my brothers and several friends have PD and if they can gain some benefit from this book, then it was well worth the time to write it. When I initially started to write this book, the only thing that I knew about Parkinson's disease was not to confuse Parkinson's Disease with Parkinson's Law. Despite my limited knowledge of PD, one salient point I hope to convey to the reader is this: spiritual music therapy with a prayer of faith and hope will calm an anxious heart, bring solace to a troubled soul, and create peace of mind, regardless of the adversities and vicissitudes to which we are confronted in this life.

After I was diagnosed with Parkinson's Disease (PD), I have attended numerous PD workshops, conferences, support group sessions, and physical therapy classes number of visits, and I have made a preponderant number of visits to medical doctors, I realized that a spiritual element of PD Therapy was neither mentioned, nor emphasized. Based upon my experience and judgment, this is a very serious omission. For this reason, I decided to address this void and write a succinct book about PD symptom, and therapies and to recommend that spiritual music therapy be included as another viable treatment afforded to PD patients. Therefore, the book should equip PD patients with enhanced resiliency to cope with PD.

COPE

The letter C stands for collaboration, generating an output greater than the sum of the parts.

The letter O stands for opportunities abound to make rational decisions

The letter P stands for planning for the future, learning from the past, and living in the present.

The letter E stands for execution with a reasonable start and with all deliberate speed.

Scripture Quote of the day:

"Choose you this day, whom ye will serve...but as for me and my house, we will serve the Lord." Joshua 24:15(KJV)

CONTENTS

CHAPTER 1

The Fundamentals of Parkinson's Disease (PD)

What is PD?

Parkinson's disease is a progressive disorder that involves the malfunction of vital nerve cells in the brain called neurons. Some neurons produce dopamine, which is a chemical in the brain that, among other functions, sends messages to the part of the brain that controls motor functions such as walking. PD is a gradually progressive degenerative disorder of the central nervous system. The disease is part of a group of conditions referred to as movement disorders. Four characteristic problems are caused by PD including:

(1) Tremor at rest
(2) Balance problems
(3) Stiffness
(4) Slowness of movement

The disease occurs when the area of the brain called the substantia Ingra is slowly destroyed. The reason for this destruction is not known currently. With some patients is seems to be occurring due to genetic, environmental, or a combination of both causes. The end result is deprivation in the brain chemical called dopamine. The purpose of dopamine is to help regulate movement resulting in rigidity and slowness of movement.

How is PD Diagnosed?

PD should be diagnosed by a medical doctor who specializes in neurology and has experience in diagnosing and treating PD patents. Ideally, the MD is a movement disorder specialist. About 50,000 are diagnosed with PD every year. Ninety-five percent of those who have PD are age of 50 and older. According to the Parkinson's disease Foundation, the most prevalent motor and non-motor symptoms of PD are discussed below.

Non- Motor symptoms of PD

Loss of taste and smell
Cognition difficulties
Depression, anxiety, and stress
Compulsive buying behavior
Memory loss

The Prevalent Motor symptoms

Forward leaning when walking at a glacial speed
Loss of range of motion
Loss of balance, causing frequent falling
Tremor
Small handwriting
Foot dragging
Frozen feet after sitting for about an hour

Do the symptoms vary for each patient?

Yes, many people have a tremor as their primary symptom while others may not. For some, the disease progresses quickly and in others it may not. Some have problems with balance. PD is a neurological disorder in which the dopaminergic system is progressively degenerating, resulting in movement-related dysfunctions such as kinesis, tremor, and rigidity as well as other symptoms that are mainly cognitive and psychological in nature. These latter symptoms often occur before the motor symptoms exist; causing mood disorders that can include but are not limited to: depression, stress, anxiety, adversity, and fear of insufficient income upon retiring. In Part 2 of the book, a separate chapter is devoted to the use of the affected limb.

Seven Early Signs of PD

1. Extremely small handwriting
2. Tremor or shaking, itching in the legs, arm, or fingers
3. Stooping over
4. Loss of smell
5. Muddled speech
6. Conspicuous consumption

The Five Stages of PD

According to Margaret Hoehn, PD consists of five stages;

Stage 1. The individual has no tremors, rigidity, slowness and paucity of movement. This stage is often missed entirely by professional health providers.

Stage 2. Bilateral involvement without impairment of balance. The symptoms include but not limited to abnormal facial expressions, abnormal speech and postural abnormalities stooping when standing or walking. The person is capable of carrying out all activities of daily living.

Stage 3. Impaired reflexes: This is evident if the person is pushed from behind and loses balance. The person is usually independent in all activities of living, dressing, hygiene and eating.

Stage 4. Fully developed severe disability: The person is able to walk only by using a walker, unassisted but is markedly incapacitated.

Stage 5. Confinement to bed or a wheelchair unless assisted. Without a caretaker to provide assistance, the person is in danger of falling with an inability to get up.

Conclusion

The motor symptoms are easily identified such as tremor, slowly walking with a forward lean and slurred speech and very small handwriting. On the other hand, the non-motor symptoms are much more difficult to identify such as stress, anxiety depression, and impulsive behavior. For this reason, the non-motor symptoms are emphasized in the following chapters in this book. We know that PD affects people in ways beyond the well-know symptoms of tremor, gait, posture and balance. Depression, stress and anxiety are very prevalent and yet are often overlooked and undertreated. Depression and anxiety have a negative stigma which prohibits some people from seeking help.

Depression is caused by imbalance in the brain and is not a sign of weakness. Exercise and counseling can be effective and medications may also be needed to restore the appropriate levels in the brain. It is beneficial and helpful for all to be well informed about the risk of depression and anxiety and their symptoms. Treating PD will ease other Parkinson's symptoms.

An individual's mood should be analyzed and should be included in a doctor's exam to ensure a comprehensive visit. State your feelings in order to recommend coping strategies.

Scripture Quote of the day:

Confess your faults one to another, and pray one for another, that ye may be healed. The effectual fervent prayer of a righteous man availeth much. (James 5:16)

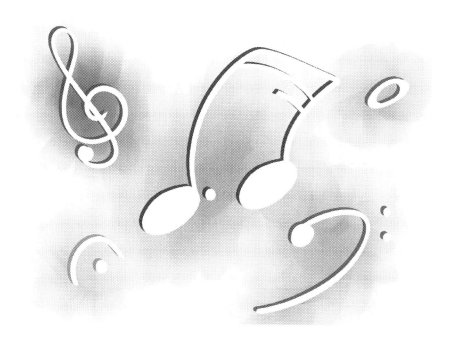

CHAPTER 2

The Basic Elements of Music Theory and Music Therapy

The origin and the basic components of Music Therapy (MT) have been used as a tool for a learning of and a feeling for a civilization's culture and language since ancient times. The writings of the Greek philosophers Pythagoras, Plato, and Aristotle validate this point. They sang their dramas because they understood how music could help them remember their lines.

Based on research by Dr. Georgi Lozanov, a renowned Bulgarian psychologist designed a way in which to teach foreign languages. His system involved using classical music with a rhythm of 60 beats per minute. He discovered that the students learned at least five times more words than the students who did not listen to background music, ceteris paribus. His students learned on average 1,000 words per day. His results indicated that foreign languages can be learned with 92% retention for his students. Student who did not listen to background music had an 82% retention rate. This study's methodology was replicated several times with different student samples, yielding the same results. Thus, gentle classical background music enhances foreign language learning and retention.

Also, Native Americans and other indigenous groups used music to enhance traditional and natural healing practices. References to music for healing have appeared in ancient Native American pictographs. Healing traditions by Chinese practitioners of medicine have used music for healing. Also, classical music in India has been used to create different states of mind for healing.

The power of music to affect memory and learning is quite remarkable. Mozart's music in the Baroque music period simultaneously trigger the left and right brain, thereby maximizing learning and retention of information. Activities that engage both sides of the brain at the same time such as playing the guitar and singing, cause the brain to be more capable of processing information.

Some scholars think that modern music therapy began in the mid 1700's when Louis Roger wrote his book, *A Treatise on the Effect of music on Body*. Others claim that the modern discipline of music therapy began after WW I.

In the early 20th century, music therapy was used to treat recovering soldiers during and after both World Wars. Patients' responses led to the growth of music therapy and generated a wider scientific curiosity an interest relative to the possible positive effects of music therapy.

What Makes Music Therapy Unique?

Music Therapy (MT) is an unconventional, multisensory therapy that is not widely adopted in medical treatment but is nevertheless, used in a variety of settings. MT is a multi-faceted branch of music consisting of psychology, theology, political science, physiology, and neurology. The primary function of MT is to enable intrinsically motivated music therapists, who are professionally trained, to use peaceful uplifting, and spiritual music to treat both non-motor and motor symptoms to include but not limited to: depression, anxiety, stress, and heart disease, all of which are associated with Parkinson's Disease (PD).

How Does Music Therapy Work?

One of the primary reasons music therapy is so effective is that music can shift the patient's focus away from a stressful event to a pleasant one by affecting physiological factors such as heart rate and hormone levels. Music therapy also modulates the nervous system and deals with psychological concerns such as depression, stress, and anxiety as well. Research has indicated that music can trigger the brain to release endorphins and block pain and increase dopamine levels to treat the symptoms of PD. Music is powerful--it moves people physically and emotionally. The chapters in part 2 of the book are devoted to explain how music therapy assists patients, who suffer both physical and psychological, from PD symptoms.

Two parts of MT

1. Active (MT) means that Music Therapy is used and considered a viable approach in healing a person with PD.

2. Passive (MT) means that there is no commitment to MT by some of the healthcare providers. In fact, some tend to feel that the Music Therapy is seemingly repugnant to the medical profession. With an active MT program, music therapy can make a significant difference. Instruments have been developed to involve all five sensory organs in order to obtain a suitable non-motor and emotional response. Active MT is the focus of this book Music Therapy is a burgeoning discipline. To become a music therapist, you must be an accomplished musician who has a fairly deep knowledge of how music can evoke an emotional response to relax and stimulate patients to heal themselves. Music therapists normally can play a musical instrument and sing concurrently, and are sufficiently competent to teach their patient's how to play and sing. College trained certified Music Therapists have few constraints. They are encouraged to be innovative and creative in helping their patients heal. For example, the Coordinator of the Music Therapy Program at Massachusetts Harvard General Hospital stated: "The favorite part is seeing how big an impact music can have on someone who isn't feeling well. Music Therapy has been applied as an integrative and complementary therapy for many disease conditions. Moreover, for most people, music is an important part of the daily tasks to get through the morning commute. Also, during a physical workout, many people will play or sing certain songs that make them happy. Thus, all forms of music may have a therapeutic effect; however, music from one's own country and culture may be more effective. For example, the Chinese medical theory is that the human being has five internal organ systems each with musical tones which are used to encourage healing.

Dr. Lee Boethius stated:"Music is so naturally united with us that we cannot be free from it, even if we so desired." Throughout history, music's spiritual interconnection with society can be seen. To this day, spiritual music in some cultures is still used for inspiration and healing as one of the basic actions and functions of culture. Because music was not handed down from generation to generation or recorded, there is no official record of "prehistoric" spiritual music. Nevertheless, there is evidence that prehistoric spiritual music was used in a variety of different purposes. Music Therapy has been used in the United States since the early 1940's. It is a spiritual value Integrated with Music Therapy.

The song of a righteous person is a prayer unto the Lord. Why? According to David Randolph's book, *This is Music* noted that music cannot be reduced to notes on a music score, or verbal and pictorial terms. Uplifting good music must be FELT as an experience. Dr. Bernie Siegel, MD, in his book, *How to Live Between Office Visits*, said "we should listen to the still small voice" (I KINGS 14:24.) Listening to the Holy Spirit empowers us to enjoy health both spiritually and physically. By living the Two Great Commandments, which can be summed up in a few succinct words: Love God and Love your neighbor as yourself; we can have the Spirit guide us and feel His peace. Moreover, by the prayer of faith, which is usually embedded with spiritual Music Therapy, we can come to know that PD or any other disease is not punishment from God. Thus, the question is not: Why me Lord? But rather the question is: why not me? What can I learn from this PD experience? Affection and disaster come with the territory in living. Opposition should never be interpreted as the Lord's punishment for not loving God or your neighbor sufficiently. One prayer we should all learn to recite is the Serenity Prayer by Reinhold Niebuhr.

Serenity Prayer

God grant me serenity to accept things I cannot change, courage to change the things I can and the wisdom to know the difference.

There should not be any doubt that this prayer is the essence of living on Mother Earth. Listening to spiritual music should open your heart and enable you to not only hear the music but also to feel the music. From the perspective of the lay listeners, the five elements of music are of somewhat limited value because listeners are usually unaware of hearing any of them separately. However, when these five elements are combined, they form an inextricable sound effect with which listeners enjoy. Clearly, the end result is a musical piece that is greater than the sum of the parts or elements of the music. For listeners to understand the relationship of contemporary music to the past music, they need to acquire some knowledge of the historical development of these primary elements. Most historians concur with the notion that music started with the beating of a rhythm. Following is an explanation of the five elements of music that are the basis on which music therapy has developed.

The Five Elements of Music

1. Rhythm

Historians have noted the close relationship of various rhythmic patterns with body movement. For example, Brazil still teaches it. Capoeira is a dance that originated in Africa whereas the black redeveloped it as a self defense. Thus, rhythm is the first of the musical elements. Many years passed before man learned how to write down the musical rhythm. It measured off into evenly distributed units as it is today. After rhythms were transcribed successfully, innovation had far reaching effects. Music was not so dependent on the spoken word. What evolved was a rhythmic structure of its own. Rhombic music was the forerunner of contrapuntal or many voiced music. The emotional impact of simple rhythms can have an electrifying effect beyond analysis. All we can do is acknowledge the powerful and often hypnotic effect of the music on the listeners and not feel so superior to the African tribesman who first developed the various complex rhythms.

2. Melody

Melody is second in importance to the five elements of music. It is associated with the mental emotions. A beautiful melody should have love, with low and high points. Most important of all, its expressive quality should arouse an emotional response from the listener. The melody is the subject matter of music. As you listen for melodies take note of their length, their characters, and their reappearances. Melody goes hand in hand with rhythm. Mono tones are boring. Most melodies are accompanied by a variety of instruments of secondary interest. Don't allow the melody to be submerged by the rhythm.

3. Harmony

In comparison with rhythm and melody, harmony is much more sophisticated. Harmony and complex rhythm and melody come to a composer naturally; however, harmony is evolved incrementally and slowly. It is derived from an intellectual conception of the mind. Harmony is probably the most original conception of the mind. It was unknown to music until the ninth century. One significant innovation occurred prior to World War II by Darius Milhaud. He introduced the idea of sounding two or more separate tonalities concurrently or simultaneously. The concept is called polytonality or today is referred to as a chord.

Ambient noise can enhance creativity, but loud music is harmful to the brain. I will address this notion in chapter 3. Really soft quiet music will calm the soul, enrich the spirit, and bring solace to the mind.

Pythagoras is better known for his mathematical theorem; however, he observed that the musical pitch of notes differed according to the different lengths of an instrument's strings. He deducted what underpinned musical harmony was as well as musical intervals. He further postulated that mathematics lay at the heart of reality--not water, not air, but numbers. The shape of objects determined the movement of the stars. He developed a thematic harmonious relationship known as music of the stars.

4. Tone Color

This refers to the quality of sound produced by specific instruments or the voice. The musical tone color is that quality of sound produced by a specific medium of musical sound. Knowing the names of the musical instruments and its quality is important. Meeting the following two objectives:

(1) Sharpen the awareness of different instruments and their separate tone of different instruments and their separate tone color.

(2) Establish brain appreciation during a concert. The basis, on which a composer chooses one instrument rather than another, is the one that best expresses tone color.

5.   Music Form

Music form tends to be elusive. To avoid any possible misunderstanding, the concept is defined by Mr. Randolph's book. Form has two applications in music:

1. Refers to the overall structure of the music relative to the multi movements of the music as is the case for a symphony.

2. Refers to the structure of each individual movement. Of the five elements of music, form usually is the least to be understood

Generally, professional musicians are more affected emotionally and more immediately satisfied by the charm of the rhythm and melody than they are to structure. Thus, for this reason, form is normally the least appreciated in musical theory.

The fundamental question to which a trained musician must broach is: Because form is an important element in music, how much theory ought to be understood by a layman in order to appreciate the music basics?

Well trained musicians could admit that form in music is above all, a means of providing aesthetic feelings to the listener, recalling music as a pleasure. Moreover, the purpose of music is to give the listener some forms of music which may not meet that expectation. That is understandable since the materials, melodies; rhythm, harmony, color, and form are essentially abstract and subjective, thereby causing sometimes pain rather than pleasure while listening to various forms of music. The musician has considerably more freedom to include abstract material than any art or literature. Consequently, musicians are less answerable to the demand of logic and community values. Attending an R-rated movie is different than an R-rated musical. What is considered to be pornographic art in comparison to pornographic music is quite different. The musicians apply the tone color they prefer which makes form specificity and generally more elusive to the listener. While comparing the relative merits of art and movies, perhaps the most formidable obstacle in music exists in time only. When you look at a painting you are able to take the entire picture at one glace. The relationship among the various colors is immediately apparent, and the form and content of a painting can be grasped almost immediately. Not so with music.

It is impossible to ascertain the idea of form and shape by listening to only the opening movement without listening to the entire piece; unlike Calculus, in which several people could be given the exact same problem to find the derivative of a given function, and must find the one and only one answer. Whereas, a group of musicians could be given the exact same parameters for music composition and comparable theme, but the composers will create entirely different musical works. Because of inherent flexibility, musicians have considerable latitude in obtaining a feeling of completeness. They can argue and dictate pervasively that there is more than one perspective shape or form possible. Music can be a significant medium to communicate feeling and emotion.

Our appreciation of music is predicated on the degree to which we comprehend the music, particularly ecclesiastical music. Music does vary according to the manner in which we were socialized, while growing up to adulthood. Particularly classical music varies with our background, education, socio-economic influences, and our personal experiences. Classical music is the basis on which Music Therapy is built.

Our mood at any given moment affects our reaction and response to the music we are hearing. Hence, the sixth element of music is the listener. To enhance the listener's understanding is the purpose of this book.

The layman should be able to differentiate three different kinds of musical texture. Three types of music texture have been developed: monophonic, homophonic, and polyphonic. Each is discussed below:

Three Music Textures

1. Monophonic Texture

Is the simplest of the three. The music is comprised of a single melodic line. No harmony accompanies the melody line. Not only all oriental cultures, but also the Greeks had a monophonic texture. In our culture, the Gregorian chant is an example of a Monophonic texture. The expressive power was enhanced greatly by the Catholic Church.

2. Homophonic Texture

Is slightly more difficult to hear the Homophonic than the Monophonic texture. It was invented by the Italian opera in the seventeenth century. Once discovered, composers became extremely fascinated with the technique.

3. Polyphonic Texture

Is comprised of several melodic strands which result in harmonies. After the year 1600, most music was written with a polyphonic structure. Music affects our feelings. Empirical research has shown that the pulse of the music can affect blood pressure and it decreases significantly to softer music. Listening to heavy metal music does cause our blood pressure rate to decrease. Pieces by Mozart can cause decrease. Thus, the degree of loudness determines our emotions. It is the basis on which various dance routines, marching bands, and etc. are composed. Our minds accept the division when change in the rhythm and the tempo occur in the musical piece. Music can communicate an emotionalism depending on the setting such as a funeral for example or football. The emotional effect of music last while we are still listening, long pause between movements or between one and the next piece can cause one to be restless and cease to listen and leave in some situations. The general agreement is that pauses should not exceed five seconds.

How Can Music Express Emotions?

When the National Anthem is played, usually patriotic feelings are evoked. Moreover, the words help to give the listeners or singers an understanding of the message that was intended. A meaningful experience is thus created.

Using Spiritual Music Therapy

On Nov 5, 2015, the Harvard Medical School posted a blog in which spiritual music therapy was explained and implemented by three different departments within the Environmental Music Program at the Harvard Medical School. Researchers reached the following three conclusions:

1. Improved invasive procedures.

In controlled clinical trials of people having colonoscopies, cardiac angiography, and knee surgery, those who had listened to spiritual music before their procedure, experienced a reduction in anxiety and a reduced need for sedatives when compared with the control group who did not listen to any music. Similar results occurred with those patients, who had listened to inspirational music in the recovery room, decreased the need for pain relief when compared with those patients, the control group, who had not listened to music. Thus, the experimental group, who had listened to music, experienced the benefit of music during and following the medical procedures.

2. Restored lost speech.

Music therapy can help people who are recovering from stroke or rheumatic brain injury who had damaged the left brain area which is responsible for speech. Because singing originates in the right side of the brain, patient's can work around the injury to the left side of the brain by first singing their thoughts and then gradually dropping the melody and begin talking. Former U. S. Representative Gabby Gifford used this technique to testify before a Congressional Committee two years after a gunshot wounded her left hemisphere of her brain.

3.   Reduced the side effects of cancer therapy.

It also curtailed nausea and vomiting for patients who had received those treatments. Listening to music reduced the anxiety associated with chemotherapy and radiotherapy treatments. A growing body of knowledge obtained by competent researchers attests that Music Therapy is more than a nice perk. It has and will continue to improve medical outcomes and quality service in a host of different ways.

The Role of Spirituality in Healthcare of Patients

Another research involved reviewing previously published studies cancer patients who were thoroughly analyzed, which included data from 44,000 patients. The basic question was: How does spirituality affect the physical, mental, and social well-being of cancer patients, going through therapy? The following results were published in CANCER, a peer-reviewed journal.

1.   Physical Health:

Patients with deep spirituality and religiousness had better health than those patients with little or no spirituality or religiousness. Better physical health couched in terms of better physical health.

2.   Spiritual Health:

The relationship of spiritual and physical health was particularly strong in patients who experienced greater emotional aspects of religion and spirituality. Moreover, patients who had a spiritual dimension in their therapy had a source larger than oneself. Researchers also added that patients, who were able to integrate their cancer therapy into their religious and spiritual beliefs, reported heightened physical health.

3. Mental Health:

The emotional aspects of religion and spirituality, rather than behavior or cognitive aspects of religion in patients were strongly linked with positive mental health. Dr. John Salsman PhD. conducted the research at Northwestern Feinberg School of Medicine in Chicago stated: "Spiritual well-being was, unsurprisingly, associated with less anxiety, decrease in depression, and lower levels of stress. Also greater levels of spiritual distress and a sense of disconnectedness with God and with a religious community were associated with greater psychological distress and poorer emotional well-being".

4. Social Health:

Social health relates to the patient's ability to engage, create, and retain social relationships during their illness. Religion and spirituality had smaller links to social health. Lead author Dr. Allen Sherman, PhD, at the University of Arkansas Medical Sciences, stated: "When we took a closer look, we found that patients with stronger spiritual well-being, possessed more benign images of God such as perceptions of a benevolent, rather than an angry or distant God, and a stronger belief such as convictions that a personal God can be called upon for assistance, reported better social health in contrast to those who struggled with their faith fared more poorly." To date this series of meta-analysis represents the most comprehensive summary and synthesis of a rapidly growing area of psychology and the role of religion and spirituality for patients and survivors managing the experience of cancer," stated Dr. Salsman. "...some patients struggle with the religious or spiritual significance of their cancer treatment, which is normal. How they resolve their struggle may impact their health but more research is needed to understand and support the patients." Thus, the conclusion of this study is spirituality plays a key role in the health and wellbeing of patients going through cancer treatment. Perhaps the same conclusion applies to patients receiving therapy for PD.

Why is MT Not Widely Accepted?

Music Therapy (MT) is not widely accepted in medical treatment. Nevertheless, it is used in a variety of settings. MT is an interdisciplinary study of which several disciplines contribute. The primary function of MT is to enable intrinsically motivated music theorist to apply a fair amount of psychology, theology, physiology, neurology philosophy, and political science to contribute to treat non-motor and motor symptoms. The reason MT is so effective is that it shifts the patient's focus away from a stressful event to a pleasant one by affecting physiological factors such as heart rate.

At the Harvard Medical hospital, a music therapist, stated: "The favorite part of the job is seeing how big an impact music therapy can have on someone who isn't feeling well." Music Therapy has been studied and implemented as an integrative and complementary therapy for many disease conditions. For most people, music is an important part of daily tasks to get through the morning commute. During a workout, many people will play or sing a certain song that makes them happy. All forms of music may have a therapeutic effect; however, music from one's own country may be more effective. For example, the Chinese medical theory is that the human being has five internal organ systems each with music tones which are used to encourage healing.

Why is Music Therapy Useful?

Music Therapy (MT) is an evidenced-based and scientifically used allied health service similar to physical therapy, occupational therapy, and speech therapy that use music as the therapeutic tool to address physical, cognitive, social, emotional, psychological and spiritual behavior needs. Music therapy is multi-sensorial therapy that is not a chemical or medical treatment. It is used to treat different symptoms of PD in a variety of settings.

(Melissa Hirokawa Neurologic Music Therapy Fellow, "Living Spirit Therapy Services, LLC, Facebook.com.).

Three Complementary Therapies:

1. Speech Therapy. Help people with PD to:

* Increase voice volume.
* Improve pronunciation and articulation.
* Enhance clarity of speech.
* Strengthen voice muscles by singing.
* Fix nonverbal communication such as facial.
* Create more face value.
* Understand speech impediments are usually part of PD.
* Start speech therapy early and perform regularly.

2. Physical Therapy. Help people with PD to:

* Increase strength, endurance, movement and control.
* Improve flexibility, gait, and balance.
* Develop a daily exercise program.
* Keep mobile.
* Relieve pain.
* Prevent or limit permanent physical disabilities.
* Help patients suffering from PD or injuries gingerly.

3. Occupational Therapy. Help people with PD to:

* Learn alternative ways which enable people to perform daily activities of life.
* Suggest ways to make a home safer and easier to help.
* Assess a person's work environment for safety.
* Collaborate with other healthcare providers.

Science vs Religion Argument

A delicate balance exists between religion and science with respect to healing. Both the sick and the robust, strong and the healthy must be enlightened on this vital aspect of life. The Music Therapy methodology focuses on building a relationship of trust between the music therapist and the patient through the application of spiritual, classical, and, soft music. This technique is the focus of this Chapter. Rehabilitative Neurologic Music Therapy is usually provided by a medical doctor who specializes in neurologology. Neurologic Music Therapy will be addressed later in another chapter.

Based on Dr.Scott Peck's book, *The Road Less Traveled*, the scientific method involves stepping back skeptically to question our basic assumptions. This can help us to discover new truths. As we become more spiritually aware, we must guard against tunnel vision where the healings and miracles are not recognized by divine intervention. By analyzing such occurrences, we can come to the understanding of a hidden truth or an answer to a vexing problem. Therefore, we must be open to the miraculous and not dismiss them merely because they do not appear to have a scientific basis.

So from where do miracles and loss emanate? Evidence seemingly points to the existence of a supreme being who loves us. God wants us to learn and grow spiritually, physically, socially and mentally; in short to be like Him. The main impediment to spur growth and love is laziness. Because love is work, the essence of no love is laziness. Most people make incontrovertible choices without pondering and facing the likely outcomes. Soft music can indeed help facilitate reflective thinking processes to engage in decisions. Decision making is pondering with quiet dignity using music as a facilitating force in decisions. Sometimes people wake up in the middle of night after pondering a weighty decision that must be made. The secret of making prudent decisions is to obtain awareness of the consequences and listen to the spirit. Sometimes you may have a feeling or a sense that they should or should not do a certain thing that results in avoidance of serious accident. Too often we tend to let small miracles pass by us because they do not fit our preconceived notions for sorting our experiences.

Thomas Aquinas spent his entire life refining a synthesis of Christian theology and Aristotelian reasoning. Aquinas's take on the science vs religion argument or reason vs. faith argument, was that "they are separate but complementary, the first subservient without being subordinate."

Spiritual Values Integrated with MT

On November 5, 2015, the Harvard Medical School posted a blog in which spiritual music therapy was explained and implemented by three different Departments within the Environmental Music Program at the Harvard Medical School Researchers reached the following three conclusions:

1. Improved invasive procedures.

A controlled clinical trials of people having colonoscopies cardiac angiography, and knee surgery, those who had listened to spiritual music before their procedure, experienced a reduction in anxiety and a reduced need for sedatives when compared with the control group who did not listen to any music. Similar results occurred with those patients, who had listened to inspirational music in the recovery room. The need for pain relief decreased significantly when compared with those patients, the control group, who had not listened to music.

2. Enhanced recovery

For those in the experimental group, who had listened to music, experienced the benefit of music during and following the medical procedures, recovering from stroke or a traumatic brain injury who had damaged the left brain area and which is responsible for speech. Because singing originates in the right side of the brain, patient's can work around the injury to the left side of the brain by first singing their thoughts and then gradually dropping the melody and begin talking. Former U.S. Representative Gabby Gifford used this technique to enable her to use the left hemisphere of her brain and speak again.

3. Reduced side effects of cancer therapy.

It also curtailed nausea and vomiting for patients who had received those treatments. Listening to music reduced the anxiety associated with chemotherapy and radiotherapy treatments. A growing body of knowledge obtained by competent researchers attests that Music Therapy is more than a nice perk. It has and will continue to improve medical outcomes and quality service in a host of different settings.

The Role of Spirituality in Healthcare

Another research involved reviewing previously published studies on cancer patients. The data were drawn from 44,000 patients. The basic question was: How does spirituality affect the physical, mental, and social well-being of cancer patients, going through therapy." The following results were published in CANCER, a peer-reviewed journal.

1. Physical Health:

Patients with a deep spirituality and religiousness had better health than those patients with little or no spirituality or religiousness. Better spiritual health couched in terms of better physical health was discovered.

2. Spiritual Health

The relationship of spiritual and physical health was particularly strong in patients who have experienced greater emotional aspects of religion and spirituality. Moreover, patients who had a spiritual dimension in their therapy had a greater sense of meaning and purpose in life, as well a connection to a source larger than oneself. Researchers also added that patients who, were able to integrate their cancer therapy into their religious and spiritual beliefs, reported heightened physical and spiritual health.

3. Mental Health:

The emotional aspects of religion and spirituality, rather than behavior or cognitive aspects of religion in patients were strongly linked with positive mental health. Dr. John Salsman, Ph.D. who conducted the research at Northwestern Feinberg School of Medicine in Chicago, stated the following: "Spiritual well-being was surprisingly associated with less anxiety, decrease in depression, and lower levels of stress. Also greater levels of spiritual distress and a sense of disconnectedness with God and with a religious community were associated with greater psychological distress and poorer emotional well-being."

4.   Social Health:

Social health relates to the patient's' ability to engage, create, and retain a social relationships during their illness. Religion and spirituality had smaller links to social health. Lead author, Dr. Allen Sherman, PhD at the University of Arkansas, Medical.

Scientists, stated: "When we took a closer look, we found that patients with stronger spiritual well-being, possessed more benign images of God such as perceptions of a benevolent, rather than an angry or distant God; and a stronger belief such as convictions that a personal God can be called upon for assistance, reported better social health in contrast to those who struggled with their faith faired more poorly." To date this series of meta-analysis represents the most comprehensive summary and synthesis of a rapidly growing area of psychology and the role of religion and spirituality for patients and survivors managing the experience of cancer," stated Dr. Salsman. "Some patients struggle with the religious or spiritual significance of their cancer treatment, which is normal. How they resolve their struggle may impact their health but more research is needed to understand and support the patients." Thus, the conclusion of this study is spirituality plays a key role in the health and well being of patients going through cancer treatment. Perhaps the same conclusion applies to patients receiving therapy for PD.

Music Therapy vs. Physical Therapy

The body and the brain respond to music with both hemispheres of the brain naturally where different musical, emotional, spiritual and physical elements of the brain are located. A person's mood can be changed by music. Dr. Alfredo Raglio performed a study in which Physical Therapy was compared with Music Therapy. Thirty-two Parkinson's patients with mild to moderate disability participated in the study. They were divided into two equal groups. Both groups went through three months of either weekly physical therapy sessions, or weekly music therapy sessions. The group that listened to music and played musical instruments, moved rhythmically with the music. The researchers discovered that the patients, who received weekly music therapy, noted that music therapy ameliorated stiffness. However, the physical therapy group stated their therapy did not have a significant, positive effect on their overall daily physical performance, whereas, the patients who received music therapy reported that their therapy not only enhanced their daily performance physically but also improved their mental attitude and intrinsic motivation.

This research was replicated in an effort to ascertain and validate the real measurable benefit of MT, in order to be considered medicine. A slight modification was done with respect to dividing the sample into two groups. One group went through three months of weekly physical therapy sessions with no music therapy; the other group experienced weekly music therapy sessions with no physical therapy. The group receiving music therapy weekly consisted off three subgroups:

1. Those who merely listened to the music
2. Those who created music by playing a musical instrument
3. Those who listened to the music and were moved with the music rhythmically. The results revealed the following:

The researchers noted that physical therapy mitigated stiffness but did not have a significant effect on daily performance, whereas those who experienced music therapy reported that daily tasks such as getting dressed or cutting meat at meals reported an improved ability to perform such tasks. Also, those who received music therapy stated that they were less likely to fall or experience the sudden freeze of their muscles. Moreover, they were happier when listening to music, thereby increasing their intrinsic motivation to move rhythmically, which is a key element in music theory.

Dr. Alfredo Raglio said: "...that the reason, music therapy is so effective is that music brings into the patient's consciousness what was previously unconscious. For example, before people had been informed that they had PD, they could ride a bike unconsciously without thinking about it. When they became PD patients, they were much more cautious. Thus, the PD patients were conscious of a motor skill task that once they could perform unconsciously. "They had moved into consciousness that which was previously unconscious." Because I am a regular mountain biker, I can validate the truth of this phenomenon. Before PD, I rode my bike without thinking twice about it. Now I am far more cautious. Following are the results of the study, indicating the power of MT. The power of MT is illustrated by the following facts:

The Power of MT

1. Reduces pain

After listening to music, patients following surgery and in recovery, experienced a significant decrease in pain. As a result, the amount of anesthesia needed during operations decreased significantly. Patients internalized neutral facial expressions. After listening to classical music participants were more likely to interpret a neutral expression as happy or sad to be in harmony with the tone color of the music. A study by Logeswaran (Long et.al (2009), found that a quick blast of happy music made participants perceive other people's faces happy. In other words, happy music caused a happy countenance; sad music caused a sad countenance. The mood of the music projected onto other people's countenance.

2. Relieves Stress, anxiety, and depression,

The patients experienced a significant decrease in blood pressure. Significant finding was the music therapy helped steady the heart rate. Our emotions are also affected by music. Two different kinds of emotions are elicited by felt emotions. The implication, therefore, is that we can understand the emotions of a piece of music without actually feeling music can be connected to the heart, mind and soul of people. Michael McLean said, "I suppose I write songs the way I do because sometimes a song can teach me the truth the only way my heart will hear it." A separate chapter is devoted to each of the above triple threats.

3.   Enhances the immune system

The patients who experienced decreasing stress hormones and increasing growth ones have a stronger resistance to sickness.

4.   Connects individuals to happiness and pleasure in the brain.

Spiritual music stimulates the same areas of the brain that trigger pleasure in other activities. Pleasurable music stimulates the mesocorticolimbic system in the brain, which is the pleasure center and which is triggered by clean humor, and tasty food. All the Christmas shows that Bob Hope organized and presented to the military, validate the fact that even in a hostile environment such as Vietnam, clean humor is great medicine for not only the audience but also for the stars participating, thus resulting in a win-win paradigm. It becomes a natural high by releasing endorphins secreted by the adrenal gland in the human body.

Group Singing Provides Satisfaction

A study reported higher satisfaction at school than those who did not participate. Singing together brings people together. One of the basic elements of music is harmony. While singing in a choir, students must listen and harmonize with other choir members so they do not create cognitive dissonance within the music. Aristotle believed that people are gregarious and need to interact. According to A. H. Maslow, satisfying the social need in his hierarchy of need theory is paramount for intrinsic motivation. Singing in a choir can be intrinsic motivation and generate great satisfaction.

Personal Experience with Group MT.

In the 1960's while in college, I played the guitar and the banjo with a few friends. As we played at some gigs, most people began singing common folk songs with us. Some of which were protest songs regarding our Country's involvement in Vietnam. Knowing about a dozen chords, you could play and sing these songs. When I visited Vietnam a couple of years ago, we sang the 60's songs once again with my guitar accompaniment, while traveling on a tour bus to Hanoi. Our guide was born and raised in Hanoi. His father was injured and was almost killed in the Vietnam War. He had served in the Communist North Vietnam Military. At the end of our tour, I shook hands with our guide and told him that I had no ill feelings or animosity toward him specifically and the Vietnam people generally. After some 50 years later, I finally, through music, made reconciliation, with both the Vietnam War and the North Vietnamese Army. I have to say that by group sing-alongs with my playing the guitar on the bus, softened my harsh feelings of ill will toward the Vietnamese people and enabled me to let the Vietnam War go, and "Let It Be" and "Let It Go." Before reconciliation, the 60's music's tone color was dark black. After reconciliation, the music's tone color changed literally from dark black to pure fresh, white as snow. Tone color is yet another very important element of music theory.

Two Brilliant Individuals Benefited from Music Therapy

1. Thomas Jefferson

Applied music therapy by playing his violin while writing the Declaration of Independence. Thomas Jefferson and Patrick Henry, both students at the College of William and Mary, became friends while doing a violin duet one evening at a fancy Christmas party. While history tells us that they both practiced obsessively, their respective talent remains questionable: One contemporary supposedly called Patrick Henry "the worst fiddler in the colonies, accepting Thomas Jefferson." This criticism could be explained by the fact that although Jefferson was fond of referring to his instrument as the more colloquial "fiddle," he probably stuck to a stately classical repertoire, and had little experience with proper, folksy fiddling. Patrick Henry, for his part, seemed to play more for his own enjoyment; visitors claimed he would play while lying on the floor as his caterwauling children crawled all over him.

2. Albert Einstein

He was an accomplished violinist in addition to being brilliant. Einstein played the violin very well. The influence of music on President Thomas Jefferson and Albert Einstein was significant. Music helped Thomas Jefferson to write the Declaration of Independence. He applied Music Therapy with his violin to help him when he was struggling for the words from his brain to write onto the paper. He is recognized as one of the smartest men who have ever lived. A little know fact is that when he was young, he did very poorly in school. His parents were told by his grade school teachers to take him out of school because he was "too stupid to learn." It would be a waste of time and money to try to educate him. His mother bought him a violin instead of following the school's advice. Einstein became a very accomplished violinist. Some suggest that music was the key that helped him to become one of the brightest in the world. Einstein himself said that the reason he was so smart is that he played the violin. He loved the music of Mozart and Bach the most. G.J. Withrow, Einstein's friend, said that the way in which Einstein figured out his problems and equations was by improvising on the violin.

Personal Experience Learning Portuguese and Guitar

I experienced a negative response from my teachers when I was studying Portuguese, prior to going to Brazil for two years to serve as a missionary. The course was an intensive program, all day and night for three months with only eating and bladder breaks. Various tests were administered each week to measure progress. During the first two months, I failed miserably all the tests, thereby causing my instructors to recommend that I go to a location where English is spoken. They would say, "The kid can't learn Portuguese". My response was, "I will learn Portuguese, even if takes two years." With spiritual help by praying, and by playing the guitar for therapy, during the third month, I started to pass the tests. My instructors were amazed. Some 50 years later, I can still speak and understand Portuguese. Remember this: "All things are possible to him that believeth."

Anapestic Rhythm and Switching

Dr. John Diamond, an Australian physician and psychiatrist, discovered that there is a direct, positive correlation between muscle strength and music. He found that all the muscles in the entire body go weak when subjected to the "anapestic beat" of music from hard rock musicians. An Anapestic rhythm consists of two unaccented syllables followed by an accented syllable. The words "underfoot" and "overcome" are anapestic. Thus, rhythm is a very critical element in music theory and music therapy. One other effect he discovered from the anapestic beat he called "switching" of the brain. Dr. Diamond postulated that brain switching occurs when the actual symmetry between the cerebral hemisphere is destroyed, causing alarm in the body, and resulting in less work performance, learning and behavior problems in children, and a "general malaise in adults." Bob Larson, a Christian minister and former rock musician, remembers well that in the 70s teenagers would bring raw eggs to a rock concert. By the end of the concert the eggs would be hard boiled by the piercing and high-pitched music sounds from the music. Dr. Earl Flosdorf and Dr. Leslie Chambers showed also that proteins coagulated from a liquid medium much quicker when subject to high piecing heavy metal, rock music is played. Therefore music therapy is critical for everyone and not just PD patients.

Implementing the Fourth Leg of a Three-Legged Stool.

Remember I introduced this notion in the preface in which music therapy would be viewed as a viable therapy for PD. treatment and the wellbeing for all who practice Music Therapy. It is absolutely paramount that the reader understands that I am not suggesting that the existing PD therapies be abandoned. Rather, keep using all the current therapies and implement Music Therapy as one more recourse and one more resource with which to treat PD. As I alluded to in the Preface, the metaphor is a three-legged stool used to illustrate the point. Each leg represents a particular therapy. To illustrate: Spiritual Music Therapy, which would be complementary and integrative therapy. The therapy package is summarized below.

Leg 1 Apply physical therapy.
Leg 2 Use doctors prescribed medication.
Leg 3 Become a member of a support group.
Leg 4 Implement Spiritual Music Therapy.

The assumption is that Mozart's music is the standard or benchmark for spiritual, inspiring music. I want to emphasize again that I am not advocating that PD patients discontinue any of the current three elements of their treatments. The notion is to keep applying the treatments in the aforementioned three areas and add Inspirational Music Therapy as a fourth component. Music Therapy is the medium through which the spiritual dimension of PD therapy is feasible. It is not without significance to emphasize that Music Therapy is complementary in nature; it is neither mutually exclusive, nor adversarial. None of the patient's existing treatments should be curtailed. The current PD treatments are to balance and to be based on and supported by a four-legged stool. I am recommending and advocating that a fourth leg be added to a three-legged stool, thereby reinforcing and buttressing the stability of the stool. Each therapy should have equal standing, in terms of emphasis, medical, administrative oversight, and importance.

This holistic methodology should not replace or preclude applying any current therapy in use or any future therapy deemed necessary and proper. This is absolutely essential.

Spiritual values

Spiritual values should be integrated with and applied by competent music therapists. Thus, a four-fold dimensional therapy could constitute a "team." Accordingly, with a collaborative and integrative work environment, a synergistic outcome should occur, whereby the end result is more than the sum of its parts, as postulated by Aristotle. Also, these four therapies should not create an opportunity cost in which a patient would have to stop one therapy, in order to apply Music Therapy. Because of impecunious financial constraints, there should neither be an increase of cost nor any trade off of one therapy for another therapy because most of the traditional three therapies could be undertaken concurrently. To illustrate this, listening to inspiring music while undergoing physical therapy is feasible. The physical therapist from whom I receive treatments, listens to inspiring, peaceful music.

Impact of Support Groups

Reciprocity and collaboration are hallmark traits when amicable decisions are consummated within a support group. What you want to avoid is conflict among the "team" players, but rather cohesion established through bonding together and by building relationships of trust. What makes music beneficial to study is the fundamental element called order. The order as compared to loud, heavy metal chaos is what makes music therapeutic. The music from the Baroque and Classical periods causes the brain to respond in special ways. This order includes singing in an outstanding way to strengthen the same muscles used for speech. Also, singing provides a way in which to improve swallowing and can decrease the problem with swallowing and mitigate issues relative to voice volume, clarity, range and fullness all of which are often problems for people with PD. For, this speech symptom, MT is appropriate.

Conclusion

MT is a viable complementary treatment for PD for the following reasons:

Both the Greek and Roman Armies used brass and percussion instruments, which are the ancestors of the cornet and tuba to convey information in the field

After the collapse of the Roman and Greek empires, martial music was preserved and refined by the Byzantine Empire. Music has a rich history in serving the military. After WWI and WWII musicians performed in military hospitals and they noticed the positive responses from the patient's. Military hospitals which hire music therapists have noticed positive effects on the patient's recovery. Also, music therapy has been used successfully to help veterans cope with the symptoms PTSD.

3. Music therapy and drugs help veterans to control and express their feelings and to connect with the music therapist.

Biblical Quote of the Day: I will sing unto the Lord as long as I live. I will sing praise to my God while I have my being. (Psalm 104.33)

Scripture of the day:

Let the word of Christ dwell in you richly in all wisdom; teaching and admonishing one another in psalms and hymns and spiritual songs, singing with grace in your hearts to the Lord.

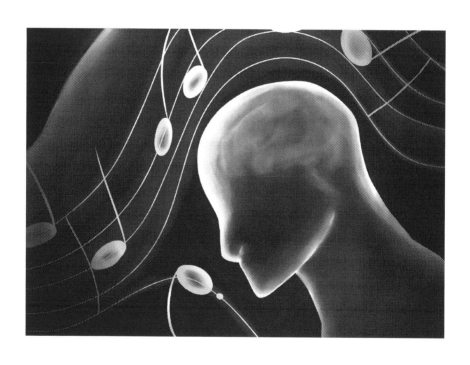

CHAPTER 3

The Elements of Neurologic Music Therapy (NMT)

What is Neurologic Music Therapy? (NMT)

Based on neuroscience research, NMT provides a specific, individualized and standardized intervention for those affected by neurologic injury or disease. NMT is different from traditional Music Therapy because NMT views music as a neuroscience model in which, music is hardwired to brain language. With traditional Music Therapy, music is viewed as a social science for the nurturing of a relationship of trust between the patient and the music therapist.

Music can impact a person's mood. For example, heavy metal music tends to prime the listener to have negative feelings, thereby causing the listener to be irritated and unhappy. Conversely, inspiring and spiritual music can have a positive influence on the person's mood and make a difference.

Three Ways Neurologic Music Therapy Affects the Brain

1. Not paying attention

According to Andrew Leung, music can affect the brain in three different ways: Music can influence how closely an individual pays attention to a task, depending on the individual's taste. Authors Rung Haw Huang et al. discovered that the type of background music and the noise level did in fact influence the listener's concentration during an exam. When the participants enjoyed the music, productivity and concentration significantly increased. When the listeners dislike the background music, productivity and concentration decreased significantly. The researchers concluded that supervisors and managers should avoid playing music that workers strongly dislike. Avoiding such music can help avoid an adverse impact on work performance.

2. Not Concentrating

The worse driving usually occurs while drivers are singing "karaoke." These types of drivers generally think that they are some rising star. Another reason for some drivers to not concentrate is that they are using their cell phones while driving. A few states have enacted legislation, making it unlawful to drive while on a cell phone. Cell phone use while driving clearly is distraction in which concentration is compromised and serious accidents can occur. Driving at night requires more concentration and is very precarious when the driver loses concentration because of being drowsy. Finally, regardless of genre, drivers who listen to loud, heavy metal music tend to be more reckless, more aggressive, more accident prone, and more likely to receive driving citations...(Warren Brodsky and Zack Sir.)

3. Interpreting

The mood of a song to which you are listening can be interpreted through the application of the five basic elements of music, which are: rhythm, melody, structure, harmony, and tone color. For example, spiritual music normally is composed with a gentle soft rhythm, peaceful melody and harmony. The mood can be changed by emotions using a different tone color. This phenomenon is called transference of emotion. Music at a funeral sets a quiet dignity mood in comparison with the music played at the half time during a football game. The auditory mood, whether sad or happy, can be projected onto another individual's countenance by transference of emotion through music. For example, a sad song at a funeral is interpreted and the perception is a sad mood. The sad mood and the sad expression are projected onto other people at the funeral by transference of emotion. The sad expression is heightened and neurological exaggerated due to how stimuli rare processed by the brain.

Spiritual Growth and Power

Power generally refers to an individual's ability to influence another person's behavior. Political power is based on and legitimized by the position held by the individual. Spiritual power emanates from the character and integrity of the leader. Spiritual music therapy should buttress political power. Based on Dr. Scott Peck's book, the *Road Less Traveled,* life is difficult. The difficulty in life itself is compounded exponentially when a person has PD. Once people accept this truth, life is no longer difficult. The reason is that once this concept is accepted as an absolute truth, the fact that life is difficult no longer really matters. Most people try to avoid confronting the problem because it is a painful, arduous and stressful process. However, avoidance behavior actually contributes to the problems and either curtails or stimulates spiritual growth. By confronting and solving our problems, we gain a greater understanding of ourselves and our place in the world. Since PD to date does not yet have a cure, PD patients must mitigate by the disease by regularly engaging in four categories of therapies: physical, mental, social, and spiritual. To walk down this road, packing the four different therapies requires self-discipline. It requires a preponderant amount of self-discipline. Effective self-discipline is predicated on the following concepts:

1. Delay instant gratification.

Being future oriented, as postulated by Harvard Political Scientist, Dr. Edward Benfield, to the extent to which the problems can be ameliorated by being patient and avoiding capricious decision making. We must understand that some decisions can be irreversible and can cause irreparable damage to you.

Dr. Herbert Simon referred to those decisions as no routine, requiring substantive research. Most weighty decisions are irreversible, incontrovertible and irreparable. Heart Simon referred to weighty decisions as non routine. A prime example of a non-routine, weighty decision would be adopting Music Therapy and Neurologic Music Therapy as a significant treatment.

2. Accept responsibility

Do not foist the blame for your personal problems onto your parents, friends, teachers, church leaders, counselors, therapist of all varieties, society, and finally God. Telling yourself because you feel that you are a sinner and not a Saint, and therefore God doesn't love you. Such a notion is a spurious claim because God is Love.

3. Believe in self-discipline

By becoming more self disciplined, you are becoming more like Christ. A disciple or a believer of Jesus Christ believes that you are a child of God the Father. Practice balancing the four dimension of your life: physical, spiritual, mental, social. All people have a religion, according to Dr. Peck, whether they formally belong to a formal church institution or not. The understanding we have of the world is our religion. You do not need to disregard everything that you may have believed to come to terms with your religious views. However, it would be prudent to analyze the source of those views and beliefs in order to validate their legitimacy.

4. Control Power and corrupt influence

Some leaders exert force in an effort to compel people to perform in a prescribed manner. However, spiritually powerful leaders inspire followers by allowing them to ponder and reflect on what lies ahead while listening to spiritual music that stirs the soul. For example, prior to engaging in Desert Storm, General Schwarzkopf played the song written by Lee Greenwood, ''I'm Proud to be an American.'' Consider another example to buttress the point. When the Mormon Pioneers were crossing the plains from Nauvoo to Salt Lake Valley, many members of the immigration party died on the trail while others suffered extreme hardships because of a harsh winter and the lack of supplies. Their leader, Brigham Young, asked William Clayton to write a song to lift the spirits of the pioneers. William Clayton responded by writing lyrics of hope and faith to an old English folk song. The song is entitled, "Come, Come Ye Saints." To this day, the song is sung with great fervor in the Mormon congregations in the language of the country in which the LDS Church is located.

The Importance of a Theistic Society

Religion provides a framework within which people can ascertain what is right and wrong; and to learn how to love God and their neighbor and thereby becoming more Christ-like. True Disciples of Christ minister to people in need and forget themselves while serving others. Thus, religion is not a one day a week exercise but rather, a seven day a week activity to learn how to love and minister to the needs of our neighbors. The word religion is derived from the Latin word religio, which means literally to tie and re-tie. Theologians have debated for years the etymology of the word religion. Thus, religion is supposed to unite and bring people together. Unfortunately, some religions have brought to society inquisitions, holy wars, intolerance, persecutions, and deaths.

Dr. Max Weber in 1904, described the loss of religious order and Christian principles in society as, "being contained in an iron cage." However, some religions in the recent past have joined together and combined necessary resources to mitigate the adverse effects of natural disasters throughout the world. Regardless of religious persuasion, some are still non-believers. The primary assumption on which this book is based is that non believers can change and become believers and the believers can increase their faith and their commitment to Christianity. Moreover, non-believers have a heart and soul and are good.

The rejection of Christian principles today is often referred to as secularism and comprised of what Freud called nonbelievers. The real intent of this book is to reinforce and buttress the belief that the Gospel of Jesus Christ is the real source of "peace on earth goodwill toward men," and can thereby, bring solace to the souls of PD patients and health care providers. To gain the most value added from the book, one must already be or willing to become a "True Believer" in Jesus Christ.

C.S. Lewis is an example of a "non-believer "in his younger years and in his later years, he made a radical change and became a "believer." He based his change on the Bible. In the preface of his book entitled *Christianity*, he wrote: "There is one God and that Jesus Christ is his only Son." He also quoted William Law: "If you have not chosen the Kingdom of God, it will make in the end no difference what you have chosen instead." According to C.S. Lewis, "Jesus Christ is the most significant reality in our world." The life of C.S. Lewis illustrates the fact that individuals can change their view about religions generally and about Jesus Christ specifically, without fear of reprisal from leaders working in government, politics, business, or educational institutions. Martin Luther king is an example, he used religion as his platform to initiate civil rights and necessary legal changes.

We should be grateful for the First Amendment in our Constitution which empowers all Americans, the right of "free exercise of religion." "We are free to choose", remember the quote by Milton Friedman. Accordingly, if consistent physical exercise is absolutely essential in treating the symptoms of PD, then consistent spiritual exercise is equally important. Spiritual exercise is complementary to physical exercise, and is just as important and essential in treating PD symptoms. Moreover, if physical and spiritual exercise is indeed complements, it seems reasonable to assume that both require discipline and commitment. Remember, the regular spiritual exercise program should not suppress a physical program, nor should a physical exercise program override a spiritual exercise program. Collaboration within your "team" is a hallmark feature. This book is written on the basis of the Gospel of Jesus Christ and our Father in Heaven's Plan of Salvation and happiness. The following scripture is the theme of the book;

"For God so loved the world that He gave His only Begotten Son, that whosoever believeth in Him should not perish, but have everlasting life." (John 3:16)

The symptoms of PD that are discussed in the following chapters can be analyzed and treated by applying the doctrines of Jesus Christ. Including spiritual musical therapy as a viable treatment for PD provides another significant resource that can be used to mitigate the symptoms of PD currently and eventually in the future result in a cure. With faith, hope, and love, and the medical and scientific community engaged with "full purpose of heart." "We shall overcome" and prevail over PD. At that point in time, science and religion will be integrated and the conflict and enmity between religion and science will be reconciled. As a member of and participant in a local PD support group, it is an excellent forum to reconcile religion and science.

Currently, the basic three types of treatments deal with and relate to the physical, mental, and social aspects of an individual. Because the spiritual dimension for PD patients usually is not addressed, I recommend that PD therapy include a spiritual component provided by a trained music therapist who is a "believer." The following chapter explains the viability of Music Therapy in treating the fundamentals symptoms of Parkinson's disease. I want to emphasize that I am not suggesting or advocating that PD patients discontinue any of the current three elements of their treatments. The notion is to keep applying the treatments in the aforementioned three areas and add Music Therapy as a fourth component. Music Therapy is the medium to enhance the spiritual aspect of PD therapy. Music Therapy is complementary and integrative in nature; it's neither mutually exclusive, nor adversarial.

As previously discussed three common complementary therapies include Speech Therapy, physical Therapy and Occupational Therapy. Notice that these three therapies deal with the physical elements of an individual, Physical Therapy obviously deals with the physical side of a person. The irony is that Music Therapy can be used concurrently with three complementary Therapies. None of the patient's' existing treatments should be curtailed. Recall that the current PD treatments are based on and supported by a three legged stool. I am advocating that a fourth leg, Music Therapy, be added to a three-legged stool, thereby reinforcing and buttressing the stability of the stool. Each leg would represent one of the four treatment elements with equal standing in emphasis and importance. The four leg stool epitomizes a holistic methodology and would not replace or preclude applying any current therapy in use. For example, a music therapist and a support group member could be used in consultation with a medical doctor. The importance of spiritual music therapy would be included and emphasized. This four-dimensional treatment methodology could be the nexus on which a support team could be established and constitute a "team." Accordingly, with a collaborative and integrative work environment, synergy should occur, whereby the end result is greater than the sum of the parts.

The trick is to balance all four therapeutic treatments which are correlated with the four components of an individual: (1) physical, (2) spiritual, (3) mental, and (4) social, advocating that a fourth-leg be added to a three-legged stool, thereby reinforcing the overall treatments. This holistic methodology should not replace or preclude applying any of the four aforementioned therapies, and the other complementary therapies such as physical therapy, speech therapy, and occupational therapy. The appropriate level of therapy depends on and is a function of the needs of the patience. Because one therapy may work well with one patient and not work with another, the therapists must be flexible and obviously prescribe what is in the best interest of the patient. Contingency Theory works well when conditions are either volatile or predictable. Thus, the application of Contingency Theory to PD is a function of, or dependent on the patient's condition. Since every patient is put together differently, the prescription must fit the patient, not to compel the patient to fit the prescription. For example, I am a believer in prayer and fasting, rigorous daily physical exercise, except on Sunday, and daily study of the scriptures. One hour before retiring to bed, I spend that hour "sharpening the saw." reading, writing, pondering reflecting, and playing the guitar.

Conclusion

Parkinson's Disease is still an unsolved Mystery. With the Lord, I feel confident a cure will be revealed through divine inspiration and scientific research.

The Elements of Music Therapy

What Is Music Therapy?

Music Therapy has been used in the United States since the early 1940s. It is a multi-faceted branch of psychology, theology, neurology and physiology. The function is to use intrinsically motivated music therapists, who are professionally trained, to use peaceful, uplifting music and/or musical instruments to treat primarily health symptoms associated with PD. Music Therapy has been used to treat a variety of ailments related to physical, psychological, socio-economic, political, and emotional conditions in an effort to promote health and well-being.

How Does MT Function?

Patients with coronary heart disease, who listened to inspiring music, discovered that their heart and respiratory rate decreased significantly. Therefore, listening to music was very beneficial therapy because their heart and respiratory rates not only decreased but also the rhythms were constant and peaceful. Moreover, this study was replicated by The Arts and quality of Life Research and discovered the same result. Just as I stated in the Preface, because the spiritual therapy dimension for PD patients usually is not addressed, I recommend that PD therapy include a spiritual component through the application of Music Therapy. The notion is to keep applying the treatments in the aforementioned three areas and add Inspirational Music Therapy as a fourth component. Music Therapy is the medium to enhance the spiritual aspect of PD therapy. Spiritual Music Therapy is complementary and integrative in nature; it's neither mutually exclusive, nor adversarial. None of the patient's' existing treatments should be curtailed. To use a metaphor, the current PD treatments are based on and supported by a three legged stool. I am recommending and advocating that a fourth leg be added to a three-legged stool, thereby reinforcing and buttressing the stability of the stool. Each leg would represent one of the four treatment elements with equal standing, in emphasis and importance. This holistic methodology would not replace or preclude applying any of the currently used levels. However, instead of lifting an individual's spirit and mood, music can destroy them, unless intervention is used. Heretofore, the intervention is normally drugs. An alternative is the application of inspiring, spiritual music. Music with all its complexity seemingly harmonizes with the complexity of PD, and changes an individual from a depressed mood to a happier one. Exactly how music calms the troubled heart has yet to be determined and is an unsolved mystery similar to finding the cause of PD. Adding music therapy to treat PD is an attempt to bring two dynamic systems together to interact and thereby changing the course of yet another system--the cure to treat PD.

When people are exposed to classical music, such as Mozart's Sonata with Two Pianos, for example, a mysterious thing happens to them. Their heart rates tend to synchronize with the music; their minds become quiet, and their thoughts melt away into the melodies. Their whole being tends to transcend time and space as they float into the harmonies and gentle rhythm of the music piece. If individuals listen to music with a faster rhythm, such as John Denver's song, "Country Roads," again something happens; they begin tapping their feet to the rhythm of the music; their pulse rate quickens; they smile; and they reflect on the happy times and memories they had experienced in the past.

Why Implement MT?

According to Dr. Richard Restak, neurologists who have undertaken a preponderant amount of research regarding the brain, discovered that music provides another means by which individuals can enhance their creativity. For instance, analysis of PET scans has revealed that the cerebellum is larger in the brains of musicians than in those of nonmusicians. The fine motor control skills needed to play musical instruments are encoded within a larger cerebellum. Thus, the cerebellum is usually larger in the brains of musicians than in those of nonmusicians. Musical knowledge learned over several years of arduous but necessary and proper practice, is stored in the cerebrum which is directly connected to the cerebellum.

Storing Information in the Brain

Based on research performed by Dr. Restak, cerebrum and the cerebellum endured musical performances. He found that the stored knowledge in the cerebrum is not stored only in a few specialised areas in the brain as believed previously, but is dispersed and interconnected to brain areas, thereby facilitating multi-tasking. For example, a musician is able to concentrate on the rhythm, melody, harmony, and lyrics concurrently. It is very important to remember that you don't have to learn to play a musical instrument to augment your brain's performance. Merely listening to spiritual and inspirational music activates the frontal lobes and limbic cortex on both sides of the brain. Conversely, music you find disturbing and unpleasant will activate a different brain area, referred to as parahippocampal gyrus on the right side of the brain. Parents with teenagers have a sound, defensible, neurological basis and reason unpleasant style of music. Because people differ significantly as to what constitutes unpleasant music, the decision is personal matter. One could respond, I know it when I FEEL it.

How to Feel Music: A Personal Experience

Since the issue of determining what is disturbing and unpleasant music is a matter of personal choice, I shall relate a personal story. While serving in Vietnam as a medic in the 8th Field Hospital, my wife mailed me a tape recording of her senior voice recital. Her recital was the capstone project to fulfill all the requirements to receive a Bachelor's Degree in music from the university to which she attended. When I played the tape, numerous people asked me all the five W's: Who is she?, What language is she singing? Where is she performing? Why is she performing? Many made copies of the entire recital. Her genre was, art songs in a variety of languages: Italian, Spanish, and German. Another personal story to buttress the notion that spiritual music therapy can have a profound impact on people, who listen with all their heart, mind, and soul, is the following. On the first date with my future wife, we attended a Protestant Church with her parents. During the meeting, my date sang "The Lord's Prayer." As I listened very attentively, I felt a spiritual shock throughout my heart, mind and soul. At that moment I knew that she would be my wife. The event occurred the same day Neil Armstrong landed on the moon. I said to myself: One small step toward marriage for Roger Lee and one leap of faith for other single males.

How does Music Therapy Function?

Gordon Shaw, a physicist and the author of the book, *Keeping Mozart in Mind*, stated the following: "The more we understand about impact of music on the brain, the more we'll see how important music is. We're aware of the emotional impact of music, but it goes way beyond that. It has an effect on the reasoning and thinking part of the brain." To support his claim, he studied college students and created two groups: an experimental and a control group. The experimental group had listened to Mozart music for a short period of time, while the control group had not listened to Mozart's music. The experimental group was significantly more efficient in solving spatial problems than the control group. Shaw replicated his research with new samples of students and reached the same conclusion. Therefore, his conclusion is not a spurious claim. Listening to Mozart's music specifically, and to classical and inspiring music generally, enhances spatial problem solving skills and nurtures internal peace of mind and solace to the soul.

The Impact Music Therapy has on the Brain

When people are exposed to classical music, such as Mozart's *Sonata with Two Pianos*, for example, a mysterious thing happens to them. Their heart rates tend to synchronize with the music; their minds become quiet; and their thoughts melt away into the melodies. Their whole being tends to transcend time and space as they float into the harmonies and gentle rhythm of the music piece. If individuals listen to music with a faster rhythm, then again something happens; they begin tapping their feet to the rhythm of the music; their pulse rate quickens; they smile; and they reflect on the happy times and memories they had experienced in the past.

The Potential Positive Effects of Music Therapy

Positive responses to music can be observed. Empirical research has generated evidence to support the claim that music influences humans both in good and bad ways. The effects are long lasting and instant.

Music is the link of the emotional (mental), spiritual, social and physical elements of the universe. Thus, an individual's mood can be changed by music. Moreover, music strengthens or weakens emotions, depending on the event. For example, music played at a funeral will elicit a sad emotion. Moreover, people respond and perceive music differently. A professional musician may hear and feel a piece of music in a totally different way than a non-musician or beginner. This is why two accounts of the same piece of music can be interpreted totally differently. Music can also vary significantly with respect to the rhythm. One response is the actual hearing of the rhythm and the other response is the physical movement of the body in cadence with the music.

Learning and Critical Thinking

Music Therapy enhances learning and thinking critically. Many leaders in a given career field learn to play a musical instrument. For example, Larry Page, co-founder of Google plays saxophone; Steven Spielberg is a clarinetist; Woody Allen performs in a jazz band; and Paula Zhan plays the cello.

The body contains a rhythm set by the heartbeat contingent upon the physical activity and the music to which the person is listening. The following research has shown that Classical music from the Baroque period causes the heart and the mind to relax to the beat of the music, thereby supporting the claim that Classical music affects deep breathing.

Researchers at the University of North Texas conducted a three-way test on randomly selected postgraduate students to determine if classical music could help in memorizing vocabulary words by relaxing the body generally and the brain specifically with Classical music. The students were divided into three equally sized groups. Each group was given three tests: a pre-test, a post-test, and test one week following the first two tests. Group 1 was to read the words with Handel's Water group in the background. They were also asked to imagine the words. Group 2 was to read the words with the same background music; however, they were not asked to imagine the words. Group 3 only read the words with no background music and no imagery. The results from the first two tests indicated that groups 1 and 2 had scored significantly better than group 3.The results from the third test, one week later showed that group 1 performed significantly better than groups 2 and 3. The conclusion is that background classical music with mental imagery will enhance memory and recall while learning.

Does Singing Enhance Speaking?

Research has discovered that 90% of the PD patients were developing voice problems. Combining vocal exercises and vocal pedagogy, there is a significant difference between voice therapy and no therapy. The experimental group was the voice, singing exercises and deep breathing with the diaphragm and the control group was the experimental group that used vocal exercises. Based on this study, there was a voice therapy approach that consisted of 2 group sessions involving vocal, speech and singing exercises. A stopwatch was used and the Visi Pitch before and after 12 treatment sessions. The results revealed the following: With a finite correction factor for multiple variable, difference in pre-post measures of maximum loudness or intensity, range (db) and average frequency or pitch (HZ) in oral reading included 12 group sessions comprised of vocal, speech, and singing exercises. There were statistically significant differences between one group that applied music therapy and the group that did not change methodology of teaching. Based on this study, vocal strengthening and vocal singing helped maintain vocal skills and can slow the vocal deterioration that frequently accompanies PD patient. Thus, the answer to the question is yes.

When PD is discussed, most people tend to think of the physical symptoms such as tremors, the loss of mobility or other motor impairments. However, coping with PD also has a tremendous adverse effect on the emotional well being of the sufferer, which many people fail to consider. Psychological symptoms include but are not limited to depression, fear, stress, anxiety, partial memory loss, and frustration, which usually occur as a result of the physical symptoms. Research has revealed that depressive episodes occur on the average with 50% of PD patients. Frequently depressive episodes alternate with attacks, the patient has the symptoms of a manic-depressive individual. Alternating emotional busts of depression and anxiety occur in about 80% of the cases. However, with a loving, musical and spiritually-oriented support one can reward the winner with a shake. (The kind you drink) Well, I defeated my primary therapist two different times; three other therapists lost. I have four shakes coming. It is not without system, many of the psychological symptoms of PD can be kept under control. PART 2 in the book is comprised of six separate chapters dealing with the social, psychological and non- motor symptoms associated with PD, The application of Music Therapy is discussed as well as other the other relevant therapies.

Regular physical and mental exercise will help keep the brain functioning normally for longer period of time. For example, consistent and different exercises can actually be fun if they are performed to music with a loyal partner. A personal example will buttress the point. I made a wager with several physical therapists, from whom I have received excellent care that I could sit against a wall, according to the proper posture, longer than any physical therapist in the clinic. Let me emphasize that the physical therapists were genuinely trying to win the contest. To add a little more entertainment, while I was sitting against the wall, I sang a song and played my long-neck 5-string banjo. The body responses to music can be observed. Music affects humans both in good and bad ways and the effects are long lasting. Because music tends to connect all of the emotional, spiritual and physical elements of the universe, an individual's mood can change dramatically. Music can also strengthen or weaken emotions from a particular event such as a playoff football game. Individuals perceive and respond to music in many different ways, depending on the listener.

What makes music beneficial to study is the classical music periods which teaches the brain to respond in special ways. Generally, responses to music can tend to be long lasting; however irreparable damage does not occur. Music links all of the emotional, spiritual, and physical elements of the universe. A person's mood can be changed by music. King George I of England studied King Saul in the Bible, and realized that Saul overcame some of his rational thinking problems by listening to special music. Accordingly, King George asked George Frederick Handel to write some special music for him that would help him in the same manner that music helped Saul. Handel wrote his Water Music to accommodate King George.

One characteristic of music is repetition. Baroque and the Classical periods of music played a theme and then repeated only one time. According to Dr. Michael Ballam, Professor at Utah State University stated that: "The human mind shuts down after three or four repetitions of a rhythm, or a melody or a harmonic progression", Furthermore, according to Dr. Ballam, "excessive repetitive music is harmful to the mind". The purpose of the study was to evaluate the effects of MT in the neurorehabilitation of PD in which PD patients participated in the research.

Each component functions best within a specific range of sounds, a natural pattern of sounds. The sound environment plays an essential role in the body. With the purpose of balancing the physical, spiritual, mental and socials dimensions of an individual's life. The external sound environment plays a crucial role with respect to the brain performing its functions of controlling the nervous system, sending and receiving billions of nerve impulses, converting signals into mental images and processing information. Sounds have a profound influence on the mental images created by the brain. Thus, the brain can change the perception and the understanding of reality. When the external sound environment is not concurrent with the rhythmic sounds of the internal environment, stress, tension and fatigue result. When one listens to music, out of sync with the frequency produced by natural sounds, the body perceives the disturbing sounds as a threat and reacts to these sounds as such.

Accordingly the 'fight or flight" response alarm is turned on and the person must decide whether to flee from the imminent threat or to enter the battle and fend off the attack. If the individual decides to engage in the fight, then the body secretes stress hormones, and adrenaline. A study in Germany discovered memory recall among heavy metal music lovers was decreased by 15 %.

Populations served by Neurologic Music Therapists include, but are not limited to: stroke, traumatic brain injury, Parkinson's and Huntington's' disease, cerebral palsy, Alzheimer's disease, autism, and other neurological diseases affecting cognition, movement, and communication (e.g., MS Muscular Dystrophy, etc) NMT encompasses neurologic rehabilitation, neuro pediatric, neuropsychiatric, neuro geriatric, and neurodevelopmental therapy. Therapeutic goals and interventions address rehabilitation, development, and maintenance of functional behaviors.

The Treatment to Attain and Maintain the Health and Well Being of People.

It is an established health service similar to occupational or physical therapy. Certain universities and colleges offer a Bachelor's Degree in Music Therapy. Music therapy is a holistic approach, whereby it focuses on the well being of the entire person, not just the part which is diseased or in distress.

Why Use Spiritual Neurologic Music Therapy"?

The Book of Psalms in the Bible is an example of spiritual music praising the Lord. Music therapy has been used as a tool of healing since the great three Greek philosophers Socrates, Plato, and Aristotle. Also, music for healing has appeared in Native American and African pictographs. Chinese medical practitioners have used music for healing for centuries.

The Significance of NMT in Understanding Sound

The human body is comprised of 87 cells, tissues, organs, and systems. Each component functions best within a specific range of sounds, a natural pattern of sounds. The sound environment plays an essential role in the body for the purpose of balancing the physical, spiritual, mental and social dimensions of an individual's life. The external sound environment plays a crucial role with respect to the brain performing. According to Dr. Enrico Franz, a neurologist at New York University emphasized that the rhythmic sounds of the internal environment causes stress, tension and fatigue with long term exposure to excessive external high intensity sounds. This can not only be physically harmful, but also lead to death if you don't ameliorate the situation. Neurologic music therapy attempts to help PD patients to cope with what PD destroys, which is the ability to move automatically, unconsciously, without thinking about. For example, a teenager can ride a mountain bike on a rough and steep terrain without thinking about it. With PD, the biker must bring into his consciousness what was previously unconscious. As regular mountain biker, I can attest to the validity of this phenomenon.

Neurologic Music Therapy Services Across the Spectrum.

Of both high and low function in patients and focuses on the following areas:

* Speech
* Language
* Sensory
* Motor and nonmotor functions
* Cognition
* Balance
* Happy or sad facial expressions

What is Music Priming?

Music priming is used to determine the effects on the brain when listening to positive music and negative music. Sad music caused the individual person to project a sad countenance unto another person. Ties are called "transference of emotion." Moreover, the researchers discovered that negative sad music is processed in the right frontal areas of the Aryan while positive music was processed in the left frontal area of the brain. One of the key elements in music is tone color. Positive inspirational music is related to the left side of the frontal area of the brain, while negative dark music is processed on the right side of the brain. Thus, the tone color of music can significantly impact the manner in which the music is processed by the brain, and thereby creates the mood of the person.

NMT is a research based system of 20 standardized clinical techniques for sensor motor training, speech and language training, and cognitive training. The treatment techniques and knowledge are based on the scientific method. The treatments provided for the following ailments include but are not limited to: traumatic brain injury, Parkinson's Disease, Huntington's disease, Cerebral palsy, Alzheimer's disease, autism, and other neurological diseases affecting cognition, movement, and communication.

The Objective of a NMT Session

The therapeutic goals and interventions address rehabilitation, development, admittance of functional behaviors. Easy session lasts about 60 Minutes, and involves a trained NMT professional guiding the patient through an interactive program of therapeutic inventions that might include playing an instrument, singing along to music, or some other activity designed for that particular patient. The results can be dramatic. The therapy can treat a range of symptoms language difficulties, and vision impairment.

NMT can be used and operated on an inpatient and outpatient basis. According to Dr. Michael That, founder of NMT and based on a study undertaken by Buffer Social, three years or more of music instrument training, students performed much better in auditory discrimination agilities and fine motor skills. They also tested better on vocabulary and nonverbal reasoning skills, which involved understanding and analyzing visual information with respect to identifying relationships, similarities, and differences between shapes and patterns. Learning to play a musical instrument helps a child develop a wide variety of important cognitive skills.

Physical Therapy vs Music Therapy

Thirty-two Parkinson's patients participated in a recent study to ascertain the benefits of music therapy. They were divided into two equal groups. One group went through three months of weekly physical therapy sessions; the other groups experiences weekly music therapy sessions.

1. Those who received weekly music training for three months
2. Those who received three months of weekly physical therapy

The researchers noted that physical therapy mitigated stiffness but did not have a significant effect on daily performance; whereas those who experience music therapy reported daily tasks such as getting dressed or cutting meat at meals reported an improved ability to perform such tasks. Also they stated that they are less likely to fall or experience the sudden freezing up of muscles. Moreover, they are happier when listening to music, thereby increasing their motivation for movement rhythmically. Enrico Fazing, MD, neurologist at New York University Medical Center, stated the reason neurologic music therapy is effective is that music bring into the patient's' consciousness what was previously unconscious. For example, before a patient had been diagnosed as having PD, they could ride a bike without thinking about it. With PD, patients have to bring into consciousness what was previously unconscious.

Cognitive Dissonance

When one listens to music, which is out of sync or has no harmony, and which is a key element in music with the frequency produced by natural sounds, the body perceives the disturbing sounds as a threat and reacts to these sounds as such. If you are reading a book and the author's theories do not seem accurate based on your knowledge, then dissonance is created in your mind.

Potential Benefits of NMT

The potential benefits of Neurologic Music Therapy include ambient noise which is not always detrimental. Supported by empirical research, ambient noise can improve creativity. Moderate noise is the sweet spot that triggers the creative juices to begin flowing. Carolyn Dobson wrote a paper for the Neurologic Music Therapy Group which is affiliated with the American Parkinson Disease Association. She stated that some neuroscience studies have shown that certain types of music stimulate the production of dopamine with PD patients.

NMT and the Importance of Rhythm

Many PD patients have problems with slowness of movement. I call it "moving at glacial speed". Music, particularly rhythm can stimulate the production of dopamine and serotonin; two neurotransmitters which are diminished in PD patients. Rhythm stimulates the patterns with the patient to establish which pattern will help with walking, balance and movement. Patients focus on the rhythm Music Therapy and uses music and rhythm to directly affect the functioning of the brain. The focus is on specific, non-musical goals that are relevant to an individual's everyday life. The resulting changes in the brain extend far beyond the normal music therapy session. While the standard Music Therapy still uses music to reach non-musical goals, it is usually focused within the social and emotional domain whereas Neurologic Music Therapy focuses directly on music and rhythm and the effect on the connections in the brain. Rhythm is another key element in music. This is the reason why new connections or neural pathways in the brain can be created. These new pathways lead to parts of the brain that are not accessible by other therapies.

Music Therapy utilizes music and rhythm to build connections and to stimulate the brain to reach functional goals, and thereby change the brain in the process. Thus, the brain and the individual are changed by music. Because of complex rhythm and chord structures, seasoned guitarist must learn new chords and new rhythms to play the music well. Having played the guitar for over 20 years, learning to play Bossa Nova will undoubtedly take another 20 years to master even though I have taken private lessons in the United States from a Brazilian as well as studying in Brazil.

Music on the Mind

Music affects many different areas of the brain. When an individual listens to music, it is processed in many different area of the brain. The extent to which the brain was involved with and affected by music was unknown until the early 90' when functional brain imaging was made possible. The major computational centre areas are shown. Individuals who had received three years or more of musical instrument training performed better than those who did not receive such music training with respect to auditory discrimination abilities, fine motor skills, vocabulary, nonverbal reasoning skills, understanding, analyzing visual information, identifying relationships, similarities and differences between shapes and patterns.

Potential Negative Effects of NMT

The drugs prescribed for a PD patient may interact and cause adverse impacts on the PD patient. My motto: "Do no harm to the patient." Accordingly this implies: First try the least invasive. Exhaust alternatives such as exercise and herbs, thereby following the spiritual route before neurologic music therapy. Also, neurologic music therapy should not be the sole therapy for PD patients. Some people may not like music therapy. Each patient is different and therefore before trying new alternative therapies, consults with a medical doctor.

Music therapy may produce altered areas of consciousness that would help discover suppressed information and skills. I have a friend who volunteered as a tutor four years in a grade school to improve the students' reading and language skills. The students manifested a positive emotional response to the volunteer and as a result, the students were stimulated and intrinsically motivated to enhance both their reading and language skills. Tutoring provided the framework while Neurologic Music Therapy interventions provided the basis for tutoring. The following skills are taught, while receiving NMT treatment:

1. Sensory Integration. Gather sensory input from the five senses are paired with specific rhythm
2. Cognition and Tension Control
3. Articulate public speaking

Play the melody of a song on the guitar; and sing the words with the right rhythm concurrently, speech imitation and sequencing. Initiate speech through speaking, chanting or singing and use specific rhythms to simulate normal speech patterns. Melody and rhythm are crucial elements of NMT.

Play an instrument with rhythmic support.

Rhythm is used to prepare the motor system for movement by an individual.

Practitioners have music for healing. Classical music in India uses melodic modes to create different states of treatment.

Research has found that music can influence the physical, spiritual, emotional, cognitive, and social well-being of the healthy, as well as for those who are ill. Later in this chapter the positive and negative effects of neurological music feedback will be analyzed. Neurological Music Therapy (NMT) may involve either listening to or performing with music with or without the presence of a music therapist. The types of music evoke different neurological stimulations. For example, classical music tends to be conducive for comfort and relaxation, while heavy metal, rock may result in discomfort for some individuals. The therapeutic effects of music therapy in part can be achieved by elevating the pain threshold amount. Research has shown that neurologic music therapy is different from the traditional music therapy. Neurologic Music Therapy based upon neuroscience, brain research that is individualized and specific intervention for those affected by either neurologic injury or disease. Music therapy consists of a music therapist and the patient working jointly develops a social relationship of trust. The therapist uses music to evoke emotional well being for the patient to cope with depression, anxiety, and stress.

The Effects on the Brain of Heavy Metal Music

The human body is comprised of 87 cells, tissues, organs, and systems. Each component functions best within a specific range of sounds -- A natural pattern of sounds. The sound environment plays an essential role for the purpose of balancing the physical, spiritual, mental, and social dimensions of an individual's life. The external sound environment plays crucial role with this balancing function. The vibrations in the human body create a natural pattern of sounds that is essential to human health and balance physically, mentally, and spiritually. The sound in ones environment plays a vital role in the agility of the brain to control the nervous system, to send and receive billions of nerve impulses, convert signals into mental assigned to process information. Exposure to external sounds that do not match or are not congruent with the rhythmic sounds of the internal environment may cause stress, tension and fatigue. When one listens to music that is out of sync with the frequency produced by natural sound, they perceive the disturbing sound as a threat and react to these sounds with the fight or flight response to prepare the body to flee from the impending threat or to enter into a battle to fend off the attack. Stress hormones, adrenaline, and cortical are secreted into the body's raising blood pressure, and cholesterol levels. These hormones are beneficial and necessary if the body is entering a battle or is under assault because they direct blood flow to the muscles in the arms and legs. Oxygen fuel the body during the physical challenge. The viscosity of the blood is increased to enable blood clots to protect the body from bleeding to death if it is wounded. This response can be saving only when it is truly needed. On the other hand, these hormones can be harmful. Endorphins can produce a state of relaxation and well being. This is how addiction to loud music begins. As individuals listen to loud music, they increase the volume higher and higher to the extent that you can clearly hear the music. A study conducted by the British Royal Academy reported that internationally, up to 75,000 young people between the ages of 14 to 24 year old have died as a result of an addition to loud blaring music.

Some Parkinson's Patients have benefited from the effects of music on the brain. Motors skills improved when some patients were better able to a walk while listening to gentle music. However, heavy metal music can cause negative effects. The heavy metal music can cause the brain to lose its symmetry between its right and left hemispheres. The rhythm and the melody and too much repetition lead to feelings of anger and hostility. Research undertaken by Jordan Taylor Sloan, a Nashville Journalist revealed that heavy rock music is literally ruining our brains.

Exercise with Background Music

Exercise and music have been studied for years. In 1911, Leonard Ayres found that cyclists pedaled faster while listening to music than they did in silence. The explanation for this phenomenon is that listening to music drowns out the brain and the music effects of anxiety cries of fatigue. When the body realizes that we are tired and want to stop exercising, the body sends a signal to the brain to stop for a break. Listening to music competes for our brain's attention and the music helps us to override the signals of fatigue.

Spiritual Values Can Benefit Society

Frequently, religious beliefs and practices are criticized as being irrational and at odds with government social goals. You do not have to be a believer to realize that the core values of Western Civilization are grounded on what is morally right. Many significant moral advances in Western Civilization have been as a result of religious principles which are preached over the pulpit. Most Parkinson's disease can affect a patient's mood, thereby causing depression, stress, anxiety, fear and compulsive behavior. Section two of the book will address these issues in various chapters. Music is powerful influence on the mind.

Emotional experiences of hearing music can increase the release of dopamine--the brain chemical lacking in PD. People with music training have a better memory, planning, problem solving, organization organizing. While playing music, multiple different areas of the brain are activated and in the long run, this results in an increase in the volume and activity of the corpus callous, the bridge that allows communication between the two sides or hemispheres of the brain.

Can Neurologic Music Therapy Mend the Mind?

Yes, the universal language of music, those who have difficulty recalling a daily schedule or conveying orally can communicate in a different manner, expressing their emotions and connecting with other people on a deeper level.

Playing Music is a Full Body Workout for the Brain.

Playing music is a complicated undertaking that engages multiple as of the brain concurrently. In essence, it's the epitome of multi-tasking. Playing music exercises the mind and body. It provides a route to social interaction and human relationships.

Make Your Own Music

If you have the opportunity, participate in a band, consider singing in a music program with a local school or church choir based upon neuroscience research. Neurologic Music Therapy (NMT) provides a specific, individualized, and standardized intervention for those affected by neurologic injury or disease. NMT differs from traditional Music Therapy. It views music not as a social science model for well being, but a neuroscience model, where music is a hard-wired brain language."

Another company that has performed a preponderant amount of research regarding neurologic music therapy is called MED Rhythms. The answer to the fundamental question: What is neurologic music theory? It is as follows:

"Based upon neuroscience research, NMT provides a specific, individualized, and standardized intervention for those affected by neurologic injury or disease. NMT differs from traditional Music Therapy as it views music not as a social science model for well being, but a neuroscience model, where music is a hard-wired brain language." I wrote the lyrics for a song to be accompanied on the guitar.

The Institute for Music and Neurologic Function (IMNF) offers music to the patients in an effort to improve their health and well being. The focus is on movement disorders. Also, the Institute helps patients who exhibit too much movement, shaking, slow rhythmic music slows down the body while peppy music help stimulate patient to "shake it up baby and twist and shout." Music therapy helps patients with articulation difficulties. Combining music with exercise is good.

Why Use Neuropsychological Music Therapy?

Neurologic Music therapy applies music, with an analysis of rhythm, as a treatment to attain and maintain the health and wellbeing of people. It is an established health service similar to occupational or physical therapy. Certain universities and colleges offer a Bachelor's Degree in Music Therapy. Music therapy is a holistic approach, whereby it focuses on the well being of the entire person, not just the part which is diseased or in distress. The physical, psychological, cognitive, social needs of people it serves, neurological, music therapy has physiological effects on heart rate, blood pressure, immune system responses, and neurologic functions. Rhythm is a concept we share with all life. Biological patterns range from simple rhythms of the heart to complex rhythms of the nervous system. From the rhythms and vibrations of atoms and molecules all matter is made. Effective people are in rhythm with their environment. Neurological Music therapy helps people with stress and time management issues; fear and neurological crisis; anxiety, debt, and depression problems; as well as motor coordination and sensory concerns.

Benefits of NMT

1. Improves verbal skills.

A study of 8 people on their musical instruments and enrolled in music classes developed higher verbal skills in comparison to those students with no musical training (Forgeard et al, 2008). Thus, the benefits of learning a musical instrument are not solely musical but extend to cognition and visual perception.

2. Mitigates heart disease.

They found that patients with heart disease who merely listened to soft music experienced a significant decrease in their heart rate, blood pressure and anxiety level. (Bradt & Dileo, 2009

3. Creates cathartic effect.

Research has shown that music can have a cathartic effect on people. Acing to Kawaka et al, (2013), sad music is enjoyable to some individuals because it creates an interesting mix of emotions, some positive and some negative. We tend to perceive the negative emotions in the music; however, we do not feel them. This phenomenon is called mood management. This is the reason people love music. It occurs only when sad music can lift you up spiritually. A prime example of this is when Joseph Smith was incarcerated in Carthage jail with his brother and couple of friends. He asked John Taylor to sing: "A Poor Wayfaring Man of Grief." After John Taylor finished singing all seven verses, Joseph Smith asked him again to sing the entire song again. Shortly thereafter Joseph Smith was killed with his brother Hyrum Smith. As Joseph Smith and his associates were en route to Carthage jail to await a trial for spurious allegations, Joseph Smith started following as transcribed by John Taylor: "I am going like a lamb to the slaughter; but I am calm as a summer's morning: I have a conscience void of offense towards God and towards all men. I SHALL DIE INNOCENT, AND IT SHALL YET BE SAID OF ME--HE WAS MURDERED IN COLD BLOOD."

Joseph Smith did not suffer from depression, anxiety or stress, which is the topic of the next chapters; rather he had a faith in Jesus Christ. Depression is a very prevalent illness associated with PD. Depression may be the most discussed psychological problem in the country. The emotional pain of depression is more severe than the physical pain of broken leg. Unlike a broken leg, however the pains of depression occur much more incrementally and gradually. Many people suffer from the symptoms of depression without even realizing that they suffer depression rather than from some purely physical illness. Unfortunately, as common as it is to hear about, depression is too often only vaguely understood. The purpose of the next chapter is to illuminate a few factors that create depression and to suggest some countermeasures that can help alleviate it.

Conclusion Chapter 3

Depression is a devastating illness that affects the total being--physically, emotionally, and spiritually.

Quote of the day

"Cast not away therefore your confidence, which hath great recompense of reward." (Hebrews 10:35-36)

CHAPTER 4

How to Cope with the Need for an Exercise Program

Physical Exercise

Seven question must be answered before undergoing a physical exercise program according to the American Council on Exercise

1. Do you have a heart condition and should you only participate in exercising that is recommended by a doctor?
2. Are you undergoing an exercise program currently?
3. Do you become dizzy and lose your balance or lose conscious?
4. Do you have a bone joint that would aggravate your legs when walking or running?
5. Do you take blood pressure or heart medications?
6. Have you experienced unexplained weight loss, in the last six months?
7. Do you know of any reason why you should not participate in physical activity?

If you answered "Yes" to any of the questions, you may want to consult with your physician.

Physical Exercise: A Ritual

Sometimes my mind is telling me, "you don't need to exercise today, you're just too busy, I need new shoes, it's too cold or too hot". Avoid negative self-talk. People with PD ought to maintain an active lifestyle as much as feasible. Research has discovered that physical activity helps to improve many PD symptoms. There is no one exercise prescription. Every PD patient is different and put together unequally. Many physical activities work well to improve mobility and flexibility example-running swimming, and jogging. The trick is to keep progressing because PD is chronic and a progressive disease. Thus, you must keep the exercise effort for long term. As the economist John Keynes said: "In the long term we all die." What type of exercise is best for PD patients? The answer depends on each individual's symptoms and challenges. My preference is mountain biking. Each summer, a "Pedal for Parkinson's" is held in Kaysville, Utah. It is great way to satisfy social need, among other things.

At the end of this chapter are numerous stretching exercises with instructions.

Consider the following reasons to take walks and exercise regularly.

1. Provides relief from nagging ailments such as stiffness and creaky knees.
2. Helps the body use glucose more efficiency and prevent a blood sugar spike.
3. Calms an overactive brain and restores attention.
4. Reduces high blood from the triple threat: depression, anxiety, and stress.

Research has shown that six different types of walkers produce different outcomes. Following are very different walkers:

1. The Family 20-minute walker

Calmed down when irate with a family member.

2. The Tree Hugger Walker

Participated with a group of walkers who walked in a forested area and another group was sent to a large urban city. After one hour, the tree hugger walkers experienced improved heart and lung functions while the city walkers did not have such improvements. Thus, Nature walks are healing.

3. The Meditation Walker

Found that meditation can lower blood pressure, improve digestive problem and ease anxiety, depression stress and insomnia. You can meditate while walking.

4. The memory walker

Memorized scriptures and poetry while walking. Researchers followed up on a 13 student study with sample of 300 older adults. They found that those individuals who walked six to nine miles a week lowered their risk of memory and cognition problems by 50%.

5. The philosopher King Walker.

Pondered and reflected on, various philosophical issues, and enhanced performance with cognitive task by 50%.

6. The Socialize Walker.

Joined a "bored, blue, and broke" support group and significantly lowered blood pressure, reduced bad cholesterol, and decreased the heart rate.

Spiritual Exercise

Does prayer create false hope? NO! Prayer is similar to medicine. A doctor prescribes medicine with the hope that it will do what it is supposed to do. Does prayer fill a void if no treatment includes prayer and divine intervention? If there is divine intervention, why is the outcome variable and sometimes totally inconsistent? There are a few medical doctors who weigh in and support Ayer and the spiritual dimension of a person. Others are like Sims Flay, a believer (his word) C.S. Lewis was a non believer in his younger years and become a devout believer in his older years. For the record I'm a believer; however, I am also a believer in medicine, and doctors. Personal stories will buttress this point.

Social Exercise

Belonging to and participating with the Davis County, Utah Support group has really been beneficial. PD patients cannot be isolated. Abraham Maslow discussed the social need in his hierarchy of needs. One of the cruelest, short of death is solitary confinement, the worst punishment. PD patients need to maintain an active lifestyle. Music has a profound effect that is connected by music. Also music activates many different parts of the brain such as: motor cortex, sensory motor cortex, auditory cortex, hippocampus, rebel cerebellum, amygdale, nucleus accumbens, and prefrontal cortex. These components can have emotional responses to the brain's reward center. Negative effects of music on the brain include a reduced ability to concentrate and memorize information. When the music evokes powerful memories, this can cause overwhelming emotional reactions in some people.

Mental exercise

1. Accept who you are and eliminate negative self-talk.
2. Connect with friends eye to eye and not just on electronic networks.
3. Learn a new skill. For example, learn to play a musical instrument.
4. Enroll in a class that reaches mindfulness. Mind your mind and expand your attitude by critical thinking.

Conclusion:

Most healthcare providers recommend physical exercise Give it a shot if you are not undertaking regular exercise programs. Always consult with your doctor before engaging in a physical program, which tends to be the most effective exercise and least costly therapy for movement.

Scripture quote of the day

"Have not I commended thee? Be strong and of a good courage; be not afraid, neither be thou dismayed: for the LORD thy God is with thee whithersoever thou goest." (Joshua 1:9)

CHAPTER 5

How to Cope with Depression

What is Depression?

A very common PD non motor symptom is depression. Many individuals do not have PD but suffer from depression. Therefore, their depression symptoms emanate from other sources in their lifestyle. Research has borne out the fact that about 60% of Americans suffer from depression. It is estimated that at least 50% of those diagnosed with PD will experience some kind of depression during their PD illness. Depression is a mood disorder in which overwhelming feelings of hopelessness impede a person's ability to function at home or work. There are many causes of depression including but not limited to the following: psychological, biological and environmental factors. However with PD patients, an imbalance of certain neurotransmitters or brain chemicals that regulate mood, play a major role and are adversely affected.

What Causes Depression?

1. Negative thoughts.

Formulate a negative attitude about living and create a feeling of hopelessness and helplessness.

2. Social Isolation.

Lack of a support group or supportive social network can make depression more probable.

3. History of mental health issues.

Research suggests that many PD patients experience depression about two years before diagnosis of PD, which suggests that depression is not only a delayed psychological reaction to the PD illness, but also part of the underlying cause of the disease process. I feel this was the case with me. My motor skills began to be adversely affected. I could not play the guitar and banjo as well. Because of poor balance, I could no longer ski as well. I was skiing with the Ski Patrol for 10 years earlier in life and really enjoyed it.

4. Changes in the brain.

PD and depression affect the same physical part of the brain that is involved with thinking and emotion. Moreover, both of these tasks, thinking and emotion affect the levels of three important and crucial PD neurotransmitters--dopamine, serotonin, and epinephrine. They influence mood and movement. I have been taking dopamine medication for 10 years with reasonable good results--not the best not the worst condition.

5. Environmental factors

Depression may occur after you have been examined by a doctor and diagnosed with chronic diseases that currently have no cure. This information was, probably the most controlling variable, causing depression for me. Furthermore, I am experiencing ongoing distress of coping and wondering how long will I be able to exercise by riding my mountain bike? I stopped running because of sore joints. I used to run half marathons. My playing the guitar and banjo is not at the comparable level that it once was. Thus, I have been compelled to alter my lifestyle pleasures, which has caused a considerable amount of distress in me.

6.   Side Effects of Drugs.

Certain prescription drugs can interact with each other and cause serious medical side effects, allergic reaction symptoms, and complications. For this reason, always consult with a medical Doctor relative to taking new prescription drugs. Doctors must be completely impartial and professional ethics precludes them from promoting specific drugs which can actually increase critical side effects. If you experience any unfavorable symptoms, contact your physician.

7.   Use a placebo

When I was in the second grade, I was a member of the Salt Vaccine Research Project. The basic purpose was to find a cure for polio. The methodology applied to test the polio vaccine was comprised of; both a Single Blind Test and a Double Blind Test in which hundreds of grade school children across the country were voluntarily asked to participate in this research study.

A Single Blind test means the doctors know who are receiving the real vaccine or treatment and who are receiving a placebo. In other words, the control group consists of children who received the placebo, while the experimental group of children received the real medicine. The primary purpose of a Single Blind Test is to control for bias with the control group, and thereby measure the significant difference between the real drug and the placebo in combating polio.

The Double Bind Test means that both the experimental group and the control group, as well as the doctors, do not know ahead of time who is receiving the real medicine and who is receiving the placebo.

Again the primary purpose is to control for bias among the doctors and the control group. By assigning a random number to each participant in the research, the doctors could track which student received the placebo and who received the real medicine, thereby enabling the doctor to evaluate if the Salt Vaccine could treat polio.

The origin of the word placebo comes from Latin and means, "I shall please." A placebo is harmless; it's given to patients to please them. For example, if a patient has a migraine headache, and the doctor prescribes a placebo and the patient believes and feels that the medicine will treat the pain, then sometimes the patient can in fact cause the pain to subside. However, if the patient still has a migraine, did the doctor violate the Hippocratic Oath? In my judgment NO, he did not violate the oath because some genuine medicine may not function properly with some patient's because of their chemical and physiological makeup. One classic example of using placebos is the Salt Vaccine Research in finding a cure to polio.

8. The common symptoms of depression

* Depressed mood
* Sleep disturbances
* Change in diet
* Fatigue
* Pleasurable activities are not appealing
* Concentration deficiency
* Low Self-esteem
* Thoughts of death

9. Alternative Treatments

* PsychoTherapy; professional counseling
* Music therapy
* Physical therapy and exercises
* Support group participation
* Cognitive Behavior Therapy (CBT).

Evidence-based Treatments for Depression.

* Change thoughts.
* Modify behaviors.
* Learn to manage depression.

Medication therapy

* Perform under the direction of a physician

Following are non-traditional and complementary therapies:

* Light therapy
* Relaxation techniques
* Massage therapy
* Acupuncture
* Aroma therapy
* Mediation
* Music therapy
* Prayer of faith
* Mindfulness

Is Prayer Good Medicine?

The answer depends on the individual you ask. A believer would most likely answer absolutely "Yes." The nonbeliever's answer would most likely be "No." A nonbeliever usually suggests that prayer is a placebo. The origin of prayer is Latin and means, "I shall please." A placebo is normally prescribed more for mental relief than for a patient's disorder. Patients think that they are receiving the prescribed medication from a medical doctor to treat a specific ailment; however, they are receiving an innocuous substance. Thus, the "placebo effect" means the improvement in the condition of a patient is in response to a placebo and not to the real prescribed medication the patient is currently taking. Therefore, improvement in the patient is due to the placebo in which the patient psychologically, spiritually, and emotionally believes his/her health condition will improve in response to the current treatment. The placebo in this example of a nonbeliever would be prayer. A prayer is offered by a believer for and in behalf of the believing patient. Assume the patient is healed. The prayer worked. The non-believer most likely would suggest that the cause and reason for which the patient was healed was that the patient and next of kin EXPECTED the prayer would work. Why would a patient ask for prayer and blessing if there only were unbelievers present? The patient had faith and belief to be healed.

Does Prayer Create False Hope?

How does a non-believer reconcile science with seemingly unexplainable phenomena such as healing? Miraculous experiences should not be dismissed merely because they do not appear to have a scientific basis. So where do miracles come from? Evidence points to the existence of a Supreme Being. Who loves us, God? He wants us to learn and grow and become like Him. What should one say and do if a prayer is offered and the patient, for whom the prayer was given, dies? Does God have bias? Does HE only answer the prayers Baptists or Jews? God is no respecter of persons.

The appropriate answer lies with Jesus Christ when He was praying in the Garden of Gethsemane and prayed saying, "Father if thou be willing, remove this cup from me; nevertheless not my will, but thine be done." (Luke 22:42) Paul taught the Hebrew that faith is the things hoped for but not seen. Faith and Hope are evidence of things not seen. Hope heals and faith mobilizes a patient's defense and assists the patient in getting well and results in specialized interventions, including the following areas in general better outcomes, initiation, executive function and body movement in a range of categories, including gait training. SEE and feel it.

How to cope with living on this planet can bring plethora of all kinds of surprises--lost 6 jobs, financial issues with the Intermountain rescue service better known as the IRS, passing out while giving a lesson in the church to which you belong one beautiful fall morning; death of a family member and death of a friend. These kinds of problems can lead to the downward spiral of depression. You go to your family doctor for an annual checkup and you are informed that you have Parkinson's Disease (PD). Medical research has validated the fact that older people are much more susceptible to medication side effects. They may discover that antihistamines, muscle relaxants, and anti nausea drugs may trigger depression. It is time to check with your family doctor to see if you have any of the following:

Serious Depression Symptoms

* Rapid weight loss or gain
* Pain in the neck, back or upper abdomen

76

* Yellowing of the eyes or skin
* Nausea and vomiting

If you have any one of the above symptoms, then you have the Lee's three B's syndrome which is: bored, blue, and broke. Life is akin to a yo-yo, life goes up and life goes down. The trick is to enjoy life regardless if your life is going down, down, down rather than going up. Three non-motor symptoms of PD play a significant role in treating PD. The three I call the "triple threats" to a person's well-being are: (1) depression, (2) anxiety, and (3) stress. Each of the three diseases potentially can really make life a struggle. For this reason, a chapter is devoted to each illness. The Music Therapy recommended in each chapter will hopefully enhance the quality of life if patient's having one or more of the three threats.

Martin Seligman described depression as "the common cold of psychiatry." About 12% of the population experience depression severe enough to require treatment. Nobody likes depression. As a result, we receive little support from others with whom we associate. Friends and relatives often will tell you "pull yourself together."

Depression is a serious PD which causes mental illness often with deep feelings of sadness and despair. Seventy percent of suffers with pre-existing anxiety tend to subsequently develop depression. Usually everybody feels sad or blue at times. But depression lasts for weeks. If your life has an unequal number of ups and downs and you have a preponderant number of downs, then here is the best to do's that I researched: If depressed for an inordinate period of time, then anxiety is on the surface. It appears that anxiety is likely to follow. The person is a victim of the three B syndromes, Bored, Blue, and Broke.

Acute SYMPTOMS follow: Treatments for SAD

1. Get an abundant sleep. You're normal if you take a 40 minute nap.
2. Avoid alcohol.
3. Manage and control yourself.
4. Talk it out with some who cares.
5. Relax, divert your mind from the everyday stresses.

6. Play a musical instrument.
7. Remember the brain smells.

The area of the brain that registers smell must also control musical emotions. This is the reason why aroma therapy and music therapy are more compatible.

Types of Depression

1. Major Depression:

  • Involves one or more periods of deep sadness, followed by a turn to normal functioning. The symptoms of major depression include but are not limited to the following:
  • Feelings of deep sadness,
  • Hopelessness,
  • Helplessness, and
  • Worthlessness.

2. Dysthymia:

Causes low moods which are less severe; however, they last for two or more years. This causes more down days than updays. The manic phase of bipolar disorder lasts at least a week and is followed by the "crash of the depression phase."

3. Bipolar Disorder:

Manic Depression relates to dramatic mood swings from intense highs to profound lows.

4. Seasonal

  • A defective mood begins in the fall and last until spring; it is triggered by reduced sunlight during the day. It is called Seasonal Affective Disorder (SAD). The Jolly Old St. Nick turns into the grumpy old Grinch who stole Christmas; the prescription is to get more light. To mitigate the lack of light do the following:

- Illuminate your sleeping area.
- Pull up the blinds and curtains.
- Distract yourself from overeating with more illumination
- Reward yourself by going to a sunny spot for a vacation.
- Learn how to apply stress management techniques.
- Study the nature of depression.
- Join a support group.

Depression is the most discussed psychological issue today. Unfortunately, as common as depression is, it is only vaguely understood. It has been reported that 33% to 50% of PD patients will experience some form of depression during their lifetime. Depression may be the most discussed psychological problem in the world. This chapter discusses a few of the factors or symptoms that cause depression and suggests some coping strategies to enable people to be proactive and ameliorate depression before it escalates. Depression, like PD, is different for each individual; however, there are a few common symptoms that are associated with depression. Generally, most depressed people are confronted with behavioral and mental issues that are beyond their ability to cope. In response, some people suffering from depression engage in activities that they think will mitigate their problems, but actually the activities are counterproductive and exacerbate their problems. For this reason, if depression is not controlled, then anxiety is likely to also become part of the same depression and anxiety escalades, and then stress enters into the problem. I refer to depression, anxiety, and stress as the "Triple Threats." In my judgment when these three diseases form a coalition, they become perhaps the most formidable battle to which an individual can confront. They are causally related to the spiral circle starting with depression. When depression increases then anxiety moves in. Now individuals have hurling tasks to perform.

Causal Anxiety Caused by Depression.

If you cut an orange in half you obviously have two pieces. Most are as the formidable "Triple Threats. As I stated in previous chapters, the illness are directly related to PD non motor symptoms for PD. The reason the "Triple Threats" are so destructive is that "Triple Threats" gang up on people. In Other words, if an individual starts to sink in the depression pit, depression will most likely cause anxiety. Anxiety and depression now can cause stress. The three deadly diseases are not mutually exclusive. The Triple Threats, depression, anxiety and stress are the most deadly diseases because the problems become more complex, irreversible, and uncontrollable.

The Symptoms of Depression

1. Thinking: Unable to concentrate.

* Inability to make rational decisions.
* Engage in self-blames and criticism

2. Feeling: Low self-confidence

* Helplessness
* Hopelessness
* Sadness
* Worthlessness
* Fatigue

3. Behaving | Withdrawal from work, people, family, and friends

* Irritable
* Loss of interest in former interests and activities

4. Changing physically

* Loss of appetite
* Loss of sleep, Insomnia

* Lack of energy
* Loss of interest in sex
* Loss of interest in family, friends, and work associates

The following behaviors are self- destructive, and counterproductive:

Ineffective Behaviors in Coping with Depression

1. Ruminating

Depressed people tend to devote tremendous amount energy toward thinking their way out of their difficult circumstances and painful feelings. Unfortunately, rather than relief, this behavior often results in an endless review of their worst experiences and scrutiny of past mistakes.

2. Critical self-reflection.

Depressed people frequently blame themselves for their difficulties, thinking that if they could just change themselves they could fix their problems. However, often ruminating over their faults, they tend to conclude that they are helpless and beyond help, leaving little hope.

3. No room for hope

The word hopeless means less hope. Thus, if people view a situation as hopeless, then the situation is beyond any further remedies. Nothing more can be under taken and the issue or problems is observed as hopeless. Nothing more can be done means all possible remedies, resources, and alternatives have been fully exhausted.

4. Withdraw from society

Depressed people often isolate themselves when they feel overwhelmed, exhausted, flawed and worthless. They think they are merely a piece of humanity. For this reason connecting with and interacting with other people is not appealing.

5. Downward spiral.

The foregoing three ingredients quickly create a downward spiral. As depressed patients ruminate, criticize, an isolate themselves, the world is lonely, and it is fruitless to try and change. This painful experience fuels more rumination.

6. Self-criticism

The result is deep depression.

7. Cognitive Impairment Depression is likely to occur in cases of severe cognitive impairment. Cognitive impairment is a very common symptom of depression. The effects of cognitive impairment include but not limited to the following: Anxiety, depression, extreme stress, excessive and impulsive behavior. The best therapy is to forget yourself and serve others. Focus on someone else. Most people spell service "self service".

8. Thinking

* Losing memory and engaging in deficit thinking
* Paying attention to and focusing on difficulties
* Experiencing remorse and motor problem such as balance
* Diminishing problem solving skills
* Having difficulty with mental calculations

9. Feeling

* Experiencing continuous depression mood
* Painful feeling, helpless
* Manifesting an unhappy, sad countenance

10. Behaving

* Redesigning activity

11. Withdrawing

12. Nurturing the mind

13. Fearing rejection

14. Eating balanced diets

15. Cognitive Problems of memory

16. Engaging in painful thinking

* Ruminating past mistakes causes pain and emotional negative self concept
* Possessing a pessimistic self-concept
* Thinking that you are a nobody
* Eating and sleeping too much, or too little
* Having an irritable disposition.

Cognitive Behavioral Therapy

Consists of three of the following fundamental principles:

1. Understand that the point of view that you "choose" is vital to your mood. The word "choose" is appropriate because as Americans, we are still "Free" to choose. Thus, our point of view is still to a large extent allowing choice, according to Dr. Milton Friedman. Our lifestyle is mostly choice-driven and not chance-driven.

2. Understand how mood and thought are linked together.

You can change your mood by first changing your thinking. Thinking and mood are dependent and not independent events.

3. Understand How to Work on both your Mood and Thoughts.

Normally you first work on your thoughts because changing your thinking you can in fact change your mood. It doesn't work well to reverse the process. For this reason a separate chapter is devoted to thinking and decision making with respect to mood.

The Basic Question

The basic question to ask yourself; Self, is there another perspective to see things? You have to answer, yes. There is always more than one way of seeing things. The challenge is to analyze other points of view and choose the best way to satisfy your need. Most people will choose their own point of view among the other choices because of ego and mental conditioning. The primary method of cognitive is to understand how to step back from your point of view and to see the facts clearly to give yourself choice perspectives. As our perspectives change, you will discover that your mood also shifts. Looking for a new and wider perspective prevents tunnel vision and getting trapped in a one-sided biased, partial, and repugnant mood. Getting the big picture and considering more alternatives or options provide you with more control over the way you feel. To describe cognitive a couple of examples should illuminate the methodology. (Dr. Viktor E. Frankl)

Dr. Frankl was incarcerated in the worst Nazi Prison camp since he was a Jew. In his book, *Man's search for Meaning*, he describes the last of human freedoms--the ability to choose one's attitude in a given set of circumstances." He did not lose the ability to choose and he chose to find meaning under such heinous conditions. Nurturing a habit of searching for more and wider perspectives helps us to cope realistically and meanful with difficulties as they occur. Cognitive equipped with a methodology that helps you to keep things in perspective.

Create Meaning to Manage Moods

* Turning your energy into art.
* Making poetry
* Painting
* Writing a book or poetry, or a song
* Building guitars, violins, banjos

How to Deal with Depression

You may feel that the problems in which you are confronted are insurmountable; however, there is good reason to feel hopeful. The majorities of depressed patients, who receive psychotherapy, take medication, exercise early regularly, sleep well, and apply Music Therapy Exercise with significant improvement. If you are still feeling stuck in depression, try doing one of the following activities:

1. Resist rumination.

2. Share your feelings.

3. Perform both physical and mental exercises.

4. Find creative outlets for your feelings.

5. Stay connected socially. Aristotle said that we are gregarious.

6. Volunteer to help economically distressed people, who live in the inner city.

7. Forget yourself and serve others.

8. Pray everyday.

9. Review goals.

10. Create objectives.

Be like Jesus: What Would He Do

1. Be open- minded

The mind is like a parachute. It only works when it is open. Depression still seems to have a stigma. If you have a broken tibia as a result of a skiing accident, you are normal. However, if you tell a friend that you are suffering from depression, the reaction is frequently quite different. Some people will have an interest in what you are sharing, while others will think that you are some weirdo who can't keep the cheese on the cracker. Remember the primary cause of depression is chemical imbalance in the brain and is not a sign of weakness or behavior abnormality.

2. Be educated

An expeditious problem response is predicated on a higher level of awareness and result is a quicker identification of the problem. Several years before I was diagnosed with PD, I noticed that my older brother had a shakes demur but I remained silent If I had raised the concern without being an alarmist, a more timely treatment and an enhanced quality of life would have resulted. Treating depression is essential while treating other PD symptoms. Failure to treat PD symptoms expeditiously usually exacerbates the problems.

3. Be happy

Some of the non-motor symptoms of PD are silent over which controlling them is a formidable challenge. However, you can and should control your mood. If your countenance looks as if you just had a hamburger with sour pickles, change the frown to a smile. Shake off the feeling of helplessness. You're in charge. Abe Lincoln's said, "most people are about as happy as they choose to be." Stoic people are not problem solvers. They don't say much and that's about what they do.

4. Be Understanding

Use empathy to really understand others.
Dr. David Burns has developed a drug free treatment for depression. "You feel the way you think".

5. Be a positive thinker

"As a man thinketh, so is he." You feel the way you think.

Let go of negative thoughts by utilizing music therapy whereby, music is used as medicine to improve the health outcomes for people with depression and Parkinson's Disease

6. Be able to apply mindfulness meditation

Mindfulness is a practice that consists of being fully engaged in whatever is going on around you. The patient ignores the everyday chatter of the mind and focus on what the body is doing. You are what you think.

The Four Steps to Implement Mindfulness:

Step 1. Find a quiet and comfortable place. Lie down on your back with your neck, back and head are straight but not stiff.
Everything is straight and in alignment but not stiff.

Step 2. Put aside all your thoughts of the past and the future. Focus on the now.

Step 3. Be aware of your deep breathing. Watch how your stomach rises and fall as you inhale and exhale. Pay attention to the way each breath changes.

Step 4. Observe how every thought comes and goes. Let eternity enter your mind; do not ignore or suppress them. Note them and remain calm and keep reacting as an anchor.
Brushing your teeth is a perfect opportunity to practice mindfulness. Feel your feet on the floor. Einstein said he did his best thinking while he was shaving. You could suggest that he was practicing mindfulness. Rather than lying down you can stand. Take the brush in your hand. Move the brush up and down and in a circular motion.

Dr. Aaron Beck developed the following four steps process to cope with depression:

Step 1. Use a diary to determine how you're spending your time.

Divide each page into one- hour increments for 24 hours. Reflecting on previous day should make you think that you did nothing much of anything. Remember Ben Franklin's axiom. "If you love life, then don't squander time. Time is the stuff life is made of."

Step 2. Rate your activities every day for mastery and pleasure. Go back over the previous day and pick out those tasks or activities that are difficult to do such as getting out of bed. Then give yourself credit if you mastered a particular task. Rate the task on a scale from 1 to ten. A rating of 8 or 9 means is difficult. A rating of 4 to 7 is moderately difficult. Rating a task from 1 to 3 is easy. Review your diary for the previous day and rate pleasure and rate pleasurable activities from 1 to 10.

Step 3. Implement Troubleshooting. Think about how to increase the amount of self-mastery and pleasure you experience. List activities or tasks that are enjoyable?

Step 4. Plan. If you fail to plan you plan to fail. Plan each day in one hour increments based on priority. Remember Goethe's quote: "Things that matter most should never be at the mercy of things that matter least."

Using Inspiring Music Therapy to Nurture Spiritual values

* Join the church choir
* Apply mindfulness
* Volunteer to teach Sunday school
* Visit members who are suffering from depression, anxiety or stress
* Serve in various capacities

Jennifer Buchanan, a Canadian music therapist, and the author of *A Music Therapy Approach to Life*, suggests that there are positive effects of Music Therapy on depression.

Bob Hope gave our troops hope for certain because he used wholesome music and clean humor. Research reveals that listening to wholesome programs like Bob Hope, gave positive results on listeners. For example, when Bob Hope visited Vietnam, the audience would laugh and laughter triggered the adrenal gland in a person's brain and created dopamine. The French Federation of Music defines music therapy as a therapeutic practice for care, support or rehabilitation in managing individuals with communication and/or relationship problems. According to Dr. Lee Bartle PhD, music professor, feels that the core of music is sound and sound is rooted in vibration. Remember the song, *Good Vibrations* by the Beach Boys? Researchers at the University of Toronto are studying if sound vibrations absorbed through the body can bare the pain from the symptoms of PD. The therapy is called fibro acoustic therapy. The intervention involves using low frequency sound, similar to a low rumble in order to produce vibrations that are applied directly to the body. While the vibracoustic therapy is being applied, the patient lies on a mat, or sits in a chair embedded with speakers that transmit the vibrations at specific computer-generated frequencies that can be heard and felt. Researchers were led by Lauren K. King of the Sun Life Financial Movement Disorder.

Wilfred Laurier University Waterloo, Ontario applied vibracoustic therapy with PD patients. The study had 40 Pseudo patients who were exposed to low-frequency 30 hertz for one minute, followed by a one minute break. They altered the two for 10 minutes which results were significant, less rigidity and better walking speed and reduced tremors. Rather than viewing music only as a cultural phenomenon, it should be seen as a vibrato stimuli that has cognitive and memory dimensions, according to Dr Lee Bart.

Pierre Lemarquis identified the effects of music on the brain. Because music emanates from emotions during music listening, this activation generates dopamine. The pain threshold is elevated with androgen released and therefore it is a safe alternative in the treatment of pain and depression. In another study the music therapy experimental group listened to music while undergoing physical exercise training and the control group received the medication secretion essential in motivations, also depressive endorphin analgesic secretion. Therefore, listening to music has a relaxing property reducing anxiety. Music's effect treating depression offers the opportunities for new aesthetic, physical and relational experiences. Music has effects on mood and emotional changes. Hearing music, singing, playing music increase attention to music and contributes to reconnect the pain with their environments. Pain is linked with society which can encompass depression and turn into anxiety. Music therapy elevates pain threshold with endorphin release. Music therapy offers a nonpharmacologic safe alternative in the treatment of depression and anxiety. In this study the music therapy group was assigned to physical exercise, listening to music versus success in the control group received therapy with antidepressant medication. The effects of the interventions were assessed by the differences changes between the two groups. The results were reduction in anxiety and in depression at three months and at six months.

Some research and hypotheses are based on the neurologic response to music. However because music is not tangible, the question is how does music stimulate the brain and create a happy mood? The answer my friend is not blowing in the wind; the answer is that music generates a unique pleasure to hearing. A feeling of love moves individuals like nothing else through emotions.

Using Herbs to Cope with Depression

Finally, remember that according to Regional's Cherry M.D. *God's pathway to healing is Herbs,* the herb most frequently prescribed for mild or moderate depression is St. John's Wort. Wort is an English word for plant. This herb is used for different mental conditions that come from chemical imbalances. Visiting members who are suffering from depression from other disease research indicates that this herb has positive effect on depression. When taking medications, you should consult your doctor to see if it will react with St. John's Wort. According to Dr. Cherry, St. John's Wort is the number one prescribed antidepressant in Germany. This herb is used for different mental conditions that occur from a chemical imbalance in the brain. It is recommended that this herb not be taken with other medications.

Two medications to assist in coping with depression and that are usually prescribed by doctors to treat depression are:

1.   Serotonin and

2. Nor epinephrine. Both medicines are extremely strong to mitigate depression; however, they are addictive analgesic. Additional non drug strategic alternatives are available:

Five Natural Strategies to Cope with Depression

1. Positive Mindfulness

Focus is on the present and is reflective rather than reactive. Moreover, it is a countermeasure to deter ruminating about the past and worrying about the future. For example, if you want to be a motivational trainer, picture yourself or picture in your mind doing that very activity. Remember, "Whatever the mind can conceive and believe, it can achieve." The situation generates intrinsic motivation a self fulfilling prophecy by your becoming a motivational speaker. Negative mindfulness is telling your brain that you are going to flunk calculus for example. And what do you do, flunk calculus.

2. Deep Breathing

Breath IN, say "Breathing in; "Breathe OUT say "Breathing out. Breathing in. Deep breathing is a gentle exercise" and the body releases endorphins, thereby getting more oxygen into the body.

3. Body Scanning

Close your eyes, and starting with your toes, you should be moving slowly. You ask yourself, "Self, where am I tense?" You should become aware of anything that is creating tension in your body. Massage the sore spot gently with your hand, thereby changing the spot from painful to pleasurable. When I started to undergo physical therapy, the therapist noticed that my face and ears were cherry red. He then realized that my breathing was very shallow rather than deep. Breathing IN and OUT causes our body and mind to be together.

4. Taste

Can you taste the difference between Coke and Pepsi?

Distraction is any activity that changes your mood from negative to positive or vice versa. You are in a situation in which you have an opposite emotion. For example you can be happy and then you attend a funeral of a close friend and now you are sad. Opposite emotions can change in a heartbeat. Another time you are driving in Rio de Janeiro, Brazil and pass numeral beaches where beautiful young women in bikinis are playing volleyball and you would like to join them is a scenario called a "sensation," an "activity" and "counting," assuming you counted the number of players. And other distraction is "contributing" by serving as a volunteer tutor at an elementary school. Most people, especially retired individuals, have a need to feel like they are contributing in order to feel good about themselves.

5. Self-Soothing: five sensory organs that are used in comforting, nurturing, and being kind are:

    1. Sight: nature, snowflakes,
    2. Sound: ocean, music forest,
    3. Smell: baking, breakfast. (See the discussion below.)
    4. Taste: soft drink
    5. Feel: the 100% silk tie

The Nose Knows

Just as antibiotics and blood pressure pills can adversely affect smell; according to Howard Hoffman, a public health expert, about 12% of adults have a smell dysfunction. With age, the problem increases exponentially to 39% of those 80 and older. People with smell deficits usually lose their sense and also lose their taste and tend to lose interest in eating. Sometimes people try to augment flour by using more sugar; potentially those people could then cause problems with high blood pressure, kidney disease or diabetes. According to Dr. Davangere at Columbia University, an expert in neurodegenerative disease and smell loss, the reason for smell loss appears to be smell deficit which can sometimes be an early sign of serious health condition such as Parkinson's Disease. For this reason, I was tested for smell deficiency twice to help assess the kind of smell disorder I had. Currently there is no treatment that is reliable and widely accepted. Training may stimulate the brain to grow new receptors but researchers are still learning how and whether this works. All the senses play an important role in a person's life. If you think you are experiencing a loss of taste or smell, contact a healthcare provider and tell him the changes in smell and taste. Cook bread or cookies if you are selling your house or a car? The sensation of smell can make it a satisfying experience. They associate yummy smells to home or back to their mom's home cooking.

A doctor who was differentiating smells said this factor is often overlooked as another symptom of PD. On October 2015, scientists investigated whether it is possible to diagnose PD by smell. The issue surfaced from a 65 year old retired Scottish nurse, Joy Milne, who claimed to have detected the onset of PD in her husband because his smell had changed. She now has been dubbed a super smeller, subtitled a"supersmeler "by the media. Although the notion seems farfetched some other diseases that kill like cancer and diabetes may be detectable by smell. This study funded by the Charity Parkinson's focused on changes in the sebum which cause an oily substance in the skin of people with condition. The change in odor seems to be a unique and subtle odor on the skin noticeable only to people with an acute sense of smell. In any case, my wife has noticed a unique odor on my skin. She is a super smeller before I was informed of this research and knowledge. She believes there are toxins in your body when someone is ill and your body is trying to rid itself of these toxins by escaping through the pores of the skin, especially when you sweat during exercise or during your sleep at night. The unique smell does appear to be valid and therefore can provide evidence to pinpoint PD. Apparently odor on the skin is noticeable by people with an acute sense of smell. Your nose knows and seemingly a correlation exists with your nose and a sense of smell and your health. Your sense of smell enriches your experience of the world around you. Various scenes can change your mood and can take you back to a pleasant memory. Your sense of smell affects your health. I was a real doubter initially when I was tested by an MD as to whether I could differentiate both the taste and smell of different odors. So what is the alleged connection between your sense of smell and your health? If your sense of smell diminished it can affect your diet, nutrition and your physical well being. When we smell breakfast for example, being cooked in the woods, the smoke from the fire smells and the things we smell are virtually tiny molecules released by substances all around us. When we breathe in deeply these molecules stimulate specialized sensory cells high inside the nose. Each sensory cell has only one type of odor receptor. Structure on the cell selectively latches onto the specific type of smelling molecule. Because there are more smells in the environment than there are odor receptors, a given molecule can stimulate combination receptors, thereby creating a unique representation in the brain of a specific smell. According to Dr. GaryBe, people vary significantly because we all have different combinations detecting cells in our noses. Two people could smell the exact same physical object and their perceptions may be very different. Aromas can affect many aspects of our lives such as memory, mood, and emotion because smell information sent to different parts of the brain. Fragrant plants have been used in healing across many cultures including China, India and Egypt for thousands of years.

Aromatherapy: Two Ways to Use it for Depression Relief

1. Candles.

Perhaps the simplest and easiest method is to burn candles with scents, thereby creating a soothing atmosphere. Unlike incense, other scents do not give off much smoke. Buy quality candles that give off a scent that is potent enough to permeate a scent around and fill the whole room.

2. Diffusers.

Diffusers are essential because they spread the scent effectively and efficiently throughout a large room without using fire or candles. Thus, they are safer than candles because they run on batteries. They are not only very aesthetically pleasing, but also, they add a soothing atmosphere with which you are trying to create.

Aroma Therapy has gained considerable attention in the recent years. Dr. Beauchamp stated that the number of aromas that people can detect surpasses 1000.

Aroma therapy products are now available on the shelves of grocery stores. Candles, herbs, essential oils, aroma therapy, and ancillary products are now sold widely in traditional grocery stores. Aroma therapy has been promoted and the question is: Does it perform the way in which is proponents' claim? That question will be addressed in Chapter 6, Coping With Stress. Although to date there is no a predominant amount of research to support the claim that is relieves stress, the notion that fond memories of smell can be vivid and long lasting which may have a positive emotional effect According to Dr. Beauchamp, Lavender has been touted as an action odor. However, is that a relationship odor because you have had past experience with this odor and have you relaxed and have you learned the relationship? Researchers are examining how different aromatherapies affected our health. Our perception of taste is also affected by smell and food releases aromas that travel from the mouth and throat to the nose. Without smelling one can only detect by taste; sweet, salty, bitter sour and savory. The brain assimilates the information from smell receptors. If the food begins to test bland some people will say they have lost their sense of taste but in fact they may have lost their sense of smell. Smell loss can be caused by a stuffy nose or a harmless growth in the nose called polyps which can block air and odors from reading the sensory cells.

Classical Music Affects the Brain to Cope with Depression

The reason why music holds such an influence is really a combination of several elements such as pitch, tempo, rhythm, loud or soft. When these elements work in combination dramatic changes in behavior occur. The positive effects of music has been documented by scientists for years and despite its mysteries, one thing is certain: listening to music activates the entire brain, thereby creating the potential for individuals to use music to improve the ways in which they think, behave, and feel. Music feeds the soul and brings people together; it is universal. Being kind for example is reciprocal. If I am kind while driving on the freeway then being kind and considerate is contagious and the person who had been treated in a big city manner will be kind to someone else. Reciprocity can be the opposite and be negative. One driver is rude and aggressive and gives other polite driver the bird, the nice driver is chafed and his emotions turn from friendly to vindictive and" let's get even" mentality. The "eye for an eye" and "tooth for tooth" philosophy has been recorded over 2000 years ago with the Jews.

Have you ever pondered how many blind and toothless people there were on the planet during that era?

Self soothing involves the whole body in which your body and mind are together. Essential oils were once considered priceless and now they are sold in grocery stores. The fundamental question is: Can Aromatherapy help relieve stress? It has not been proven as a stress reliever. However, preliminary research illustrates that aromatherapy can alter brain waves and behavior. Research has shown that aromatherapy can reduce the perception of stress, increase contentment and decrease levels of control.

One study showed that aromatherapy massage can have some beneficial effects with anxiety and depression. Moreover, a massage with aromatherapy provides a stronger and more continuous relief from fatigue, especially mental fatigue than a massage alone. While aromatherapy might not be the solution for depression, anxiety and stress, the three "Triple Threats" it is an excellent tool for depression, anxiety and stress relief. It eases any side effects, and can be used passively in a room with the lavender scent while you attend to other tasks. Also aromatherapy can easily be combined with other stress relievers such as soft music, massage, or meditation.

Two Ways to Use Aromatherapy Anxiety Relief (Summary)

1. Candles.

Perhaps the simplest way to burn candles that create a soothing atmosphere is to buy quality candles that give off a scent that is potent enough to generate a scent around the whole room.

2. Diffusers.

"These are essential" posted Eva, because they spread the scent effectively and efficiently without using fire or candles. Thus they are safer than candles because they run on batteries or are electric; they are very aesthetically pleasing as well, thereby adding the soothing atmosphere that you are trying to create.

Conclusion

1. Remember that stress and depression are not a form of punishment from God.
2. Understand God's gift to all of us. What we do with it is up to us.
3. Pray daily, ponder and reflect on the blessings you have received
4. Do some type of physical works or exercise daily except on Sunday.
5. Listen to or play peaceful music daily.
6. Forget yourself and serve others
7. Refuse to play the victim game
8. Exercise at least three times a week; Ride a bike
9. Biking works well for both the physical and mental exercise
10. Apply aromatherapy,
11. Implement the use of mindfulness
12. Engage in deep breathing
13. Include Music Therapy for treatment
14. Establish good sleep hygiene including a set bedtime and wake up time.
15. Get exposure to adequate light during the day.
16. Go for a day hike; Create a normal circadian rhythm which is a consistent time to go to bed.

God grant me serenity to accept the things I cannot change, courage to change the things I can, and wisdom to know the difference.

Scripture of the week

"So that we may boldly say, The Lord is my helper, and I will not fear what man shall do unto me." (Hebrews 13:6)

How to Cope With Anxiety

What is Anxiety?

Anxiety is an emotional response to stress; Stress is the body's physical response to excessive demands. This chapter focuses on anxiety and the following chapter deals with stress.

Feeling nervous about being nervous? If so, you are not alone. More people suffer anxiety in the United States than any other mental health problem.

Do you want to be apathetic and say, or think "All is well in Zion." According to Harvard Professor Ichiro, "if you are prone to worrying every day, then you are about four times more likely to die of heart failure than people who aren't anxious. Remember anxiety is a common non-motor symptom of PD. It is one of the "Triple Threats."

Anxiety is not merely a reaction to a diagnosis of PD, but is a part of the disease itself. The cause of the disease is in the chemistry of the brain. It is estimated between 25% to 45% of the people with PD experience an anxiety disorder. Depression and anxiety can be more disabling than any other mental health issue. Anxiety can be more disabling than the motor symptoms of PD. Anxiety is not a progressive disease but it is very common when people are diagnosed with PD. It can begin before a PD diagnosis or develop much later. While some individuals with PD experience anxiety they are also diagnosed with anxiety along with depression. The National Parkinson Foundation's Patient Outcomes Project has found that two non-motor symptoms, depression and anxiety play a key role in the diet disease as well and its effect on people's quality of life. Up to 25% to 45% of PD patients will experience some form of anxiety. Being worried about a Parkinson's diagnosis is understandable, however feelings of constant worry or nervousness is not understandable and is more serious. Remember anxiety can interfere with memory storage, disrupt attention, and can adversely affect task performance. For example some students go blank when taking a school exam when they are feeling anxious. However, the most significant impact is on the student's social life if they are not accepted by their peers. They tend to isolate themselves, and often avoid social functions, thereby causing a negative impact on family and work relationships.

Fight or Flight

Actually anxiety is a healthy and normal response that contributes to your body's fight or flight response. Moderate and normal anxiety can compel you to prepare for a quiz-a-roo or an employment interview long as you don't choke. People with a chronic anxiety for six months or more may cause a panic disorder. An example of this is Post Traumatic Stress Syndrome which some military personnel may experience (POST TRAUMATIC STRESS SYNDROME.) I have had flashbacks of my being in a Field Hospital in Vietnam as a first response to injured persons. I witnessed much trauma. These flashbacks have occurred over the years.

The Three Categories of Anxiety Disorders

Diagnostic and The Statistical Manual of Mental Disorders

1. Anxiety disorders. Usually start suddenly with a sense of pain and distress. Individuals may feel as though they cannot breathe. These episodes normally last a few minutes to an hour.

2. Obsessive-Compulsive and related disorders. People having this disorder are plagued by unwelcome thoughts. Obsessions are the urgent need to engage in certain rituals. Compulsions are for example, people may

be obsessed with germs and consequently washes his/her hands numerous times through the day. By performing these rituals the person receives temporary relief.

3. Stressor-Related Disorders. The following chapter will address stress and stressors. This differentiation of anxiety shows that while the anxiety disorders have some commonality and are related, they are distinctly different thereby requiring therapy to be necessary and proper medicine for the particular types of anxiety. In other words, one therapy is usually not compatible or appropriate for the different types of anxiety. What works for one patient may even have an adverse effect on another patient.

Symptoms of Anxiety

*   Excessive fear because of an uncertain future
*   Uncontrollable or unwanted thoughts of fear
*   Feeling overwhelmed
*   Sleeping disorders
*   Sudden flash of terror
*   Nightmares
*   Ritualistic behaviors
*   Sleeping disorders
*   Pounding heart
*   Cold and sweaty hands
*   Dizziness
*   Nausea
*   Dizziness
*   Movement disorders, disabling
*   Panic attacks
*   Phobias
*   Freezing episodes
*   Gait difficulties
*   Worrying about PD medicines wearing off

Sleeping disorders

PD symptoms include the following:

* Difficulty going to sleep and staying asleep
* Talking out loud while asleep
* Dreaming

What to Avoid

* Alcohol
* Caffeine and other stimulants such as coffee and nicotine
* Heavy exercise within six hours of bedtime
* Discussion at or before bedtime about taxes
* Clock watching

Develop a Ritual to Cope with Insomnia

• Establish a regular bedtime and morning awakening time
• Differentiate between fatigue and sleepiness.
• Turn off the TV. Rarely is the late night news soothing or relaxing.
• Limit datetime power naps to a 40-minute NASA nap
• Maintain a relatively cool room temperature.
• Banish all animals from your bed.
  • Keep lighting dim and use a nightlight to curtail falls.

Cognitive Remedies, Therapy for anxiety

* Be aware of PD medications.
* Provide counseling called Cognitive Behavioral Therapy
* Apply Music Therapy.
* Do mind and body exercises regularly.
* Implement six points of Contextual Therapy.
* Teach the patient what to compensate for their memory and thinking.

* Identify cognitive strengths that can be used to help overcome other areas.
* Tell the patient strategies that can help with anxiety.
* Create a supportive environment to express concern and frustrations.

Instructmental functioning

* Use a Neuropsychological Music Treatment when appropriate.
* Find someone who is trained in Cognitive Remediation Therapy.
* Exercise regularly.
* Implement the six Points of Contexture Therapy, as Postulated by Dr. Zane.

Seven Points of Contextual Therapy by Manuel Zane

Point #1

Expect, allow and accept that fear will arise. An individual's biological makeup of past experiences, certain thoughts and situations can automatically trigger a fear reaction. Also a fear reaction can occur spontaneously out of nowhere if the person has a panic disorder without a phobia. In either case, rather than trying to fight the spiraling process of anxiety, the mind recognizes the fears and permits the fear to be there. The person does not try to escape but accepts it and learns how to keep the fear from running his or her life. I had an experience that illustrates point.

Point #2.

One evening I was returning home, the construction workers on the freeway began closing two lanes, leaving one lane open. Several semi trailers were all trying to move over to the open lane as well as several cars. The semi truck would not let me enter to the open lane. I either could hit the truck or the closure barrels. I chose the barrel. Based on this one experience, when I see semi trucks on the freeway, I get white- knuckles and sweaty. However, I still drive on the freeway with semi trucks.

Point #3

Fear or anxiety arises usually when you expect the worst possible problem.

Accordingly you begin to think about escaping from the anticipated disaster. You either wait or run. This situation is called the fight or flight syndrome. Each time you prefer waiting rather than running, this further reinforces your confidence in trusting that by waiting, rather than running, the expected dangerous situation will pass.

Point #4

Focus on and do manageable things in the present. Focus on what might happen as opposed to what is happening. Therapies include, but are not limited to the following: talking, walking, singing counting, and riding a bike.

Point #5

Discover what make your anxiety increase or decrease. To gain an understanding and perspective of point # 4 label your level of fear from 0 to 10. Monitor your level of fear to ascertain your anxiety at any given time. Fear is not static but rather very volatile, depending on the situation in which the individual is confronted.

Point #6

Function with fear. Understand that functioning with fear creates an opportunity to achieve an experience in which there is no reason to withdraw, but rather an opportunity to learn.

Point #7

Expect and accept that fear will reappear. All learning is an up and ongoing process. Recidivism means people revert back to their old habits and thinking.

The Adverse Effects of Anxiety and Worry

Thinking

*   Interferes with concentration
*   Makes you pessimistic

Behavior

*   Interferes with performance
*   Makes you rely more on others and less on yourself

Feelings

*   Makes you feel apprehensive and fearful.
*   Makes you feel out of control and overwhelmed

Body

*   Reduces your ability to relax and sleep well
*   Makes you tense
*   Gives you headaches

Coping strategies for persistent and inordinate numerant of patients

Two types of events for which worrying is of no value and ludicrous:

1. Events that you cannot do anything about. Let worry go. Worry be gone.
2. Events that you can do something about. For example, if you are worried about an upcoming quiz-a-roo (midterm exam) in

a college course, you can study and review. If you are prepared, then you have no worries. Thus worry and anxiety are good if they compel you to take appropriate action.

The Decision Worry Tree

It is a structured paradigm to ameliorate the problem in which you are confronted. The Decision Worry Tree is predicated on the premise that you ask three sequential questions. This is what you ask yourself: self

1. What am I worried about?
2. Is there anything that I can do to mitigate the identified inherent situation?
3. Is there anything I can do right now?

The Worry Tree enables you to pinpoint succinctly the problem and whether you can do something now or defer to a later time to redo. Research has borne out the fact that about 90% of the upcoming events for which people worry do not actually occur. Their worrying is for naught. They sit in the rocking chair busily "working" and going nowhere fast. The concern is causing you to worry.

A Few Additional Non-Drugs for Treatment of Anxiety

1. Crowding Out Effect

Because the brain has a limited capacity, you can only give full attention to one thing at a time. By keeping yourself busy, your ideas fully occupied, thereby leaving no room for worry. Information overload may cause you to ignore what really matters and focus on things that are not significant and really don't matter. "Things that matter most should not be at the mercy of things that matter least."

2. Worrying at night

Worries tend to pop into your head when you are most vulnerable. You must say to yourself. "Self this is not the time to worry."

3. Boxing Your Worries

This technique was taught at a Parkinson's seminar that I attended. Imagined putting on boxing clothes and taking on extra worrying and knocking it right out of your mind. It may appear slightly eccentric, but it does feel good to vent out especially some frustrations which you encounter as an agent of Parkinson's disease PD.

4. Set-aside worry time

Put all your worries or (problems and issues) in a gunny sack and deal with each one at the appointed time and place. After the matter is resolved, throw away the matter, one by one. Then place the new worries in the gunny sack for later. You will become the "gunny sack problem solver." As you solve a problem, reward yourself with something you like. I prefer ice cream, "slide down easy" as I call it. It does work well even in the cold.

Tips for living an abundant life

*   Control moods
*   Laugh more
*   Go to the grocery store after eating
*   Pray more earnestly
*   Render service daily
*   Be cheerful and happy
*   Make peace

Conclusion of Anxiety generally but not Anxiety Disorders

1. Be aware of depression, stress, anxiety and the treatments.
2. Exercises regularly. Refer to Appendix discussing various exercises.

3. Serve others with a big smile.
4. Educate yourself about PD and its symptoms, including anxiety.
5. Find and participate with a support group.
6. Realize what symptoms can change.
7. Use treatments that work for you.
8. Be Flexible. You will never get bent out of shape if you remain flexible.
9. Keep a journal of mile stones and gallstones.
10. Figure out what sets off your anxiety or depression.
11. Apply music therapy.

Coping with Anxiety disorders

What are Anxiety Disorders?

Anxiety disorders are a very serious mental illness which causes worry to linger and become worse overtime. It is normal to be anxious at times; however, anxiety disorders tend to stay with the individual and consequently, they have a very negative and intrusive impact on a person's quality of life over the long term.

Types of Anxiety Disorders

Several types of Anxiety disorders exist:

* Panic disorder
* Specific phobia
* Social, anxiety disorder
* Post traumatic stress disorder (PTSD)
* Obsessive-compulsive disorder OCD)
* Generalized anxiety) (GAD)

As previously stated in this chapter, the newest Diagnostic and Statistical Manual of Mental Disorders (DSM-5) disaggregates anxiety disorders into three categories:

1. Anxiety Disorders
2. Obsessive-Compulsive and Related Disorders, and
3. Trauma Stressor Related Disorders. This differentiation illustrates that while the disorders have a commonality and are related, they are distinctly different as well.

Anxiety Disorder Symptoms

* Difficulty sleeping
* Feelings of panic, fear, and nervousness
* Drury, tightness, dry mouth, nausea
* Duskiness
* Nausea
* Dizziness
* Uptightness
* Tingling and numbness in the hands and feet
* Racing heart
* Rapid irregular heartbeat

Fight vs Flight decision response

Fight or Flight reaction activities are the physical and psychological resources necessary to deal with the potential danger.

Diagnosing an Anxiety Disorder

No lab test exists to diagnose an anxiety disorder. A MD doctor or a psychologist and a psychiatrist use specific diagnostic tools and questions to determine what sort of disorder the patient may have. Moreover, the fight or flight will be further discussed in the following chapter.

Anxiety Disorder Treatments

Anxiety disorders can be treated with a variety of options including the following:

1. Psychotherapy
2. Medication
3. Exercise
4. Music therapy
5. Coping strategies such as swimming
6. Cognitive-Behavior Therapy (CBT)

Discovering the necessary and proper treatment can take an inordinate amount of time, and thus usually becomes a trial and error process.

Conclusion

To be mentality fit, you need to develop the following ten fundamental skills:

1. Manage yourself with a strategy in which music therapy is implemented.
2. Identify, face, and solve problems.
3. Treat yourself properly, with respect to diet, exercise, and sleeping habits.
4. Keep things in perspective through the application of Cognitive Behavior Therapy.
5. Develop Self Confidence.
6. Relax physically, spiritually, and mentally.
7. Focus on the present.
8. Understand the past and don't let it be a burden.
9. Accept the uncertainty of the future.
10. Adopt a regular exercise program.
11. Pray daily, and acknowledge the hand of God in your life.
12. Meet with your support group regularly.
13. Forget yourself and serve others regularly, volunteer.

14. Eschew evil and the Poor Me Syndrome.
15. Implement a MUSIC THERAPY PROGRAM

* Learn from the past.
* Plan for the future.
* Live in the present.

Scripture Quote of the day:

"Is any among you afflicted? Let him pray. Is any merry? Let him sing psalms." (James 5:13)

CHAPTER 7

How to Cope with Stress

What is Stress?

Stress emanates from a variety of sources, which are called stressors. One example is a change in a job. This is a stressor to some people; however, others may look at a job change as a new opportunity and challenge. Thus, an experience considered stressful is created by our perceptions of what we encounter in life as stress, such as a change in your life. An event is stressful to some because of their perceptions of what is stressful.

The Nature of Stress

The third element of the "Triple Threats"

Recall the first element is depression, followed by anxiety and stress. Today many people experience stress but may not be able to identify what is causing them to feel stressed out. The difference between stress and anxiety is stress is a response to real situations while anxiety usually lacks a clear or realistic cause or condition that has already occurred.

Stress is a complex phenomenon and has been defined in many ways. Stress is the body's physical and psychological response to changes in living. Examples of such changes could be working at a new job, attending college after being away from college for several years, going through a repugnant, irritable, hostel, carnal, sensual, capricious and devilish divorce.

You become a believer in Thomas Hobbes advocate. These changes in a person's life are called "stressors." Because there is no way to avoid stress, it has an upside and a downside which means stress can work for you or against you. Stress management techniques within this chapter can ameliorate the downside of stress and work for you. Before addressing stress management, it is crucial that you understand the "stress response." The stress response is part of a larger response known as the "General Adaptation Syndrome" The adaptation syndrome consists of three steps:

1. alarm,
2. resistance; and
3. exhaustion

The adrenalin gland and our nervous system control and regulate the initial response. This is called the "fight or flight" response. The fight or flight response is triggered by reactions in the brain which causes the pituitary gland (the master gland) to release a hormone that protects the person. To defend yourself, the first phase is called the alarm phase. It is rather short. In the second phase, the resistance phase, the individual continues to determine to fight or flight from a situation. The resistance phase also produces a protein enriched hormone that fortifies the person. Phase three, the exhaustion phase, if prolonged, places a tremendous load on organs of the body especially the heart, adrenal glands, and the immune system. In the exhaustive phase, after prolonged stress, a total collapse of the critical body function will occur. The vital function of the body will shut down.

A Healthy View of Stress

Hans Selye, M.D. is considered the Father of Stress Management. According to Dr. Selye, stress in and of itself should not be viewed as a negative factor. It is not the stressor that determines the response, but rather the individual's internal reaction that triggers the response. This internal reaction is highly individualized as to whether the event is stressful or not. The following quote in Dr. Selye's book succinctly summarizes his frame of reference.

No one can live without experiencing some degree of stress at times. You may think that only serious disease or intensive physical or mental injury can cause stress. This is false. Cross a busy intersection, get exposed to a draft or even sheer joy are enough to activate the body's stress mechanisms to some extent. Stress is not even necessarily bad for you; it is part of living, for any emotion, any activity, could cause stress.

There is no way to avoid or eliminate stress. This is why your goal should not be to eliminate all stress, but to eliminate unnecessary stress and effectively manage it. There are some common causes of stress or stressors that many people experience; however, each person is different in coping with stress.

What is stressful?

Fact is: One person's stress trigger may not register as stressful to somebody else. That being said, some situations tend to cause more stress in most people and they increase the risk of burnout. For example, an employer may foist unreasonable demand on an employee without providing the necessary resources and time within which to complete the task. For this reason job burnout is becoming more prevalent. The "fight or flight" becomes the only decision paradigm. An individual's personality seems to be, available resources, habits can cause stress to be very unpredictable.

The Effects of Stress

Four Types of stress:

1. Physical
2. Emotional
3. Spiritual
4. Physical stresses

(1)   Physical

A result of physical exercise is generally acknowledged to be good if undertaken in moderation. Physical exercise is generally very good for you and is to be encouraged with appropriate precautions. Unless an exercise is extraordinarily excessive, physical stress does not cause heart deterioration. A sedentary lifestyle constitutes a major risk for coronary artery disease. Moveover failing to stay active is a fundamental issue with PD patients who have severe motor skill problems.

(2)   Emotional stress

Retinal stress is usually the out outcome of depression and anxiety. The mechanism by which stress can contribute to heart disease is now being elucidated. Most physicians believe that emotional stress effects heart disease in two ways. First, most people, who experience chronic emotional stress, are more likely to develop atherosclerosis, leading to coronary artery disease, stroke, and artery disease. Second, periods of intense stress tend to precipitate acute heart problems such as heart attacks (Richard N. Foghorns, MD March 29, 2016). It is very important to realize that not all emotional stress is the same and not all of it is good for people.

(3)   Spiritual Stress

One explanatory style of bad events happening to us is displacement. When bad things happen, we can either blame ourselves or internalize the outcome or we can blame God and displace our anger.

Symptoms of Stress

Stress is perceived in different ways. Stress affects us all in ways that are unique to all of us. Some people may experience headaches, while others may have an upset stomach. Stress can affect immunity, which can affect our general health. An individual's mood is affected by stress in a variety of ways as well. If you're experiencing symptoms that are related to stress, it is essential that you work on managing stress to safeguard your health.

Symptoms that may be exacerbated by stress are not "all in your head." They must be taken seriously.

Serious symptoms are:

* Anxiety
* Headaches
* Stomach pain
* Sleeping problems
* Anxiety
* Expression
* Anxiety disorder

Viable Coping Strategies for Stress

We all find different ways of coping with stress. Some strategies may emphasize stress management because response for stress wears down overtime and are temporary distractions. Not all strategies will work for every person. It's like buying a car; try several until you find one that works for you. Practice the techniques until they become habits.

Following are specific stress management techniques:

• Taking deep breaths, using diaphragm
• Listening and playing music; using Music Therapy
• Playing an instrument
• Writing about things that bother you daily for about 10 to 15 minutes.
• Letting your feelings out
• Talking
• Laughing
• Crying and expressing anger
• Engaging in a hobby that you enjoy.Try:

* Gardening, making crafts, or volunteering
* Praying daily
* Exercising regularly

Two techniques merit further explanation:

1. Reframing your situation.

Frequently we tend to intensify stressful situation by the way in which we look at them. If you can look at your situation differently, you may put the situation into a different perspective--hopefully one that causes less stress. Remember the phrase: It could be worse. Emotional stress can be caused by pessimism, Type A people.

2. Applying Progressive Muscle Relaxation. (PMR)

Release all of your muscle groups, leaving your body to feel more relaxed after.

Seven stress relievers

1. Take power naps (40 minutes).

If you are drowsy, take a 40 minute nap as recommended by NASA. Astronauts researched the optimal duration of naps.

2. Use visualization

Practice mentally whatever is stressing you, before performing.

3. Exercise

Exercise at least three times per week and undertake stretches after warming up

4. Practice deep breathing and exercises regularly. Use deep breathing.

5. Apply Progressive Muscle Relaxation in which you relax all muscles until the body is completely relaxed.

6. Implement Music Therapy. Research has validated that Music Therapy assists in mitigating stress.

7. Stay organized. Every item has a place and a place for every item.

Measuring the Level Stress

One useful survey instrument was developed by Holmes and Rah. They put a numeric value for different events that occur in an individual's life. For example, three events such as Christmas are considered to be 12 units; unemployment and divorce could be 10 and 12 points respectively, or to someone else they could be totally different. Christmas could be 6 to someone else. The higher you are the worse the stress consequences. The questions are binary, yes or no answers. The "mean value "referred to as "the Social Readjustment rating scale indicates whether you are in a major distress condition, moderate stress condition or less stress which is extremely low stress. The major concern is that Christmas may not cause a 12 point stressor condition whereas it might cause a 30 point stressor to someone else. Refer to the questionnaire on the following page. Christmas stressors might be 5 points to some, because we are all put together differently. It is a formidable challenge. Hutsomunous may rate Christmas 34 points. The points measure the extent to which a particular event is a stressor. The questions are both reliable and valid. Add up the actual numbers 12, 24 etc. from a random sample of 100 people. Take the survey and randomly pick five events that changed your life. For each stressor or unit write down the mean quantity, for example Christmas could be 12 points, getting married could be 50 points, and going on a vacation could be 12. Add these up and you get 74. A score of over 300 points indicates that an individual's chances of experiencing a health change will be very high (nearly 90%).

Personal Strategies to Cope With Stress

* Join a support group
* Exercise daily
* Apply music therapy
* Eat well
* Sleep well
* Use Music Therapy
* Physical Therapy
* Speech Therapy
* Massage Therapy
* Acupuncture Therapy
* Aromatherapy
* Meditation therapy

Exercise has been found to be very effective for improving mood and anxiety itself and coping with stress. People who want to pursue a complementary treatment for stress should be sure to visit a skilled and qualified practitioner.

As many as two out of five people will experience stress as they develop a stress management plan.

Nine adverse effects of stress:

Scientific research has indicated that the single most crucial and significant list of stress is it increases the probability of a heart attack. Following are the adverse outcomes of extreme stress and how to deal with them.

1. Affects your memory and concentration. Write things down on your cell phone, ipad, android or piece of paper
2. Makes planning and decisions difficult. Allow sufficient time in the morning or the previous evening to plan your day.
3. Causes people to become tired and fatigued. Eat quality food for breakfast, lunch, and dinner. Exercise daily for at least 20 minutes.

4. Slows down recovery hours of sleep each night. Get into a habit to sleep at least 7 hours. Lower your resistance to illness.
5. Increase your speed of recovery from illness and increase your resistance to illnesses.
6. Compels people to clarify their goals and objectives and values.
7. Determines what is urgent and important and what is not urgent.
8. Tempts you to procrastinate difficult tasks and perform the more difficult activities in the morning when you are energized by a quality breakfast with 8 hours sleep.
9. Reduces both your efficiency and effectiveness.

Become more efficient by doing things quickly and more effective by doing the right things. The foregoing seven effects can be addressed by the following; develop a stress management plan by managing yourself and your time.

Strategy to manage and minimize stress

1. Confront the problem.
2. Treat yourself right with proper sleep and physical exercise and activities.
3. Do the right things, as Peter Drucker postulated.
4. Do things right
5. Create a problem solving strategy.
6. Keep things in perspective. "Thing that matter most should never be at the mercy of things that matter least."
7. Build self-confidence from cognitive therapy.
8. Learn to relax.

Conclusion

Develop an effective Stress Management Program

1. Create Positive coping strategies
2. Get a good night sleep

3. Stabilize blood sugar levels through diets
4. Nourish your brain and body
5. Plan and organize your life

Find the Optimal Performance Zone through Life's Skills.

1. Breathe deeply from your diaphragm like an opera singer.
2. Appreciate and be grateful for what you have
3. Apply music therapy
4. Love and appreciate yourself.
5. Smile; it adds to your face value.
6. Delete what does not work for you.
7. Learn to say no without feeling guilty.
8. Realize and accept what you can't change.
9. Learn from the past, plan for the future, live for the present.

Anxiety Disorders

Five Types of Anxiety disorders:

1. Feelings of nervousness, recurring thoughts, worry and fear characterize disorder. Physical symptoms that may include, but not limited to nausea, trouble breathing and anxiety disorder usually start suddenly with a sense of pain and distress. Individuals may feel as though they cannot breathe. These episodes normally only last a few minutes to an hour.
2. Social Anoxia, piety fear of embarrassment at having PD symptoms such as tremors, foreword posture, or dyskinesias.
3. Post traumatic stress disorder (PTSD) people in the military that are in combat are vulnerable. If they have traumatic flashbacks when they return home, they should file a claim with the Veterans Administration. Some flashbacks can be related to the Vietnam war. have personally had some flashbacks of the Vietnam. War.
4. Ophidiophobia phobia, which is afraid of snakes.
5. Common biological factors

Individuals with PD can be a result of a combination of factors, including but not limited to, changes in the brain's structure and natural chemistry as well as ongoing stressful experiences that occur as a result of living with a progressive disease. Following are some 6. Common psychological factors that may contribute to the development of an anxiety disorder in PD:

Psychological Factors

1. Fear of being unable to function independently.
2. Fear of not being able to contribute to society.
3. Fear of becoming a family burden.
4. Fear of running out of money
5. Fear of feeling like a fifth tit on a cow

Biological Factors

1. Many of the brain pathways and chemicals affected by PD are the same as those in Alzheimer's disease.
2. People with P.D. have abnormally low levels of the brain chemicals.
3. Anxiety and depression are linked to low levels of this chemical, dopamine, as well.

Anxiety disorders are a serious mental illness that causes significant worry and fear. It does not go away and it may even get worse over time. Sometimes we all feel anxious; however, with an anxiety disorder, the anxiety is fairly constant and has a very intrusive and repugnant effect on a person's quality of life.

Anxiety Disorder Treatment

* Mind exercise therapy *Exercise regularly
* Cognitive Behavioral therapy (CBT) patience
* Meditation
* Music therapy

Consider Counseling, called Cognitive Behavioral Therapy (CBT)

Anxiety often is experienced by individuals who are nervous or worried about something in the future; the event usually has not happened and may never happen.

Everyone gets anxious from time to time in response to stressful situations in the future. However, if a person starts to experience persistent bad thoughts on a daily basis, then it is time to seek professional help. The primary difference between depression and anxiety is that anxiety is focused into the future; the world will end in 2020 for example. Depression occurred in the past; a person went through a divorce. Stress is related to the present for example, a person has too many irons in the fire. The National Foundation has found that two non-motor symptoms--depression and anxiety play a vital role in PD in affecting patient's quality of life.

Why Worry?

Can anything good occur because of worrying? Yes sometimes. For example, you may be worrying about an upcoming quiz-a-roo in calculus. Thus, you may be more motivated to study and prepare more diligently. Even though prayer in public schools was ruled unconstitutional by the Supreme Court, in the Case Engel vs Vitale, I witnessed students either talking to dummies or praying for divine intervention while I was proctoring the exam. Nevertheless, there is one compelling reason why worrying is so difficult to stop is that some individuals still think some good will come of it. Even when our fears are seemingly justified, the worrying seldom helps in causing a favorable outcome. As Montaigne, the French Philosopher, succinctly stated: "My life has been full of terrible misfortunes most of which never happened".

Following are situations or contingencies where worrying may be appropriate:

Contingency 1. DANGER

A siren goes off and you are under a Red Alert with incoming mortar rounds from the enemy in Vietnam. Frequent occurrences could result in

Post Dramatic Stress Disorder; a more mild situation could be when your fuel light on your car goes on.

Contingency 2. ACTION

You have an upcoming job interview. Even with your Ph.D. you have been laid off for almost one year. You are married and have five kids and it's Christmas season. Result is that you prepare for the interview by rehearsing the interview in your mind.

Contingency 3. COPING

What if I don't get the job from Contingency 2. What is my strategy to make money for Christmas gifts?

Contingency 4. LESSER OF TWO EVILS

If I don't get the job in Contingency 3, I apply Contingency 3 and 4 and cope by working at a department store during the Christmas holidays, start home-based resume and career planning business and teach courses at a local college at night as an adjunct instructor. Thus, sometimes worry is therefore helpful and sometimes makes you feel better and starts you to think about how to cope. In short it motivates and compels you to action.

Five Ways to treat Anxiety with Music Therapy

1. Listen to music daily. You can individualize your music by selecting musical instrument that you enjoy.
2. Listen to a variety of music rhythms. To relax play soft slow relaxing music and energize yourself by playing upbeat music.
3. Use technology to listen to music. Use a tablet, an iPod or headphones to block out the noise around you so that you can concentrate.

4. Attend Live Music Performances. Watching performances on T.V. is almost like being there.
5. Write a song. Sometimes it is easier to express your feelings by composing a song.

Why is Music Therapy effective in treating Anxiety?

1. Music can shift an individuals' focus from an uncomfortable event to something pleasant and soothing based on current research.
2. Music triggers the brain to enhance a sense of wellbeing. Moreover, music therapy can block pain. Research has also discovered that music therapy benefits people who have suffered depression without side effects.
3. Music therapy treats anxiety. A single blind study was undertaken in which 30 patients neither received nor listened to music. The other 30 patients did listen to music for about an hour daily. After 60 days, the experimental group experienced lower levels of medications necessary to treat anxiety attacks and chronic pain.

Conclusion

1. Do not worry; it's akin to seating in a rocking chair. You stay busy but end up going nowhere.
2. Apply Music Therapy daily faithfully. Read the scriptures.
3. Exercise daily, except on Sunday for at least 45 minutes.
4. Pray Daily and ponder and reflect on how you have been.
5. Forget youself and serve others.
6. Use the appropriate herbs to treat anxiety.
7. Attend church of your choice regularly.

Scripture of the day:

"For God hath not given us the spirit of fear, but of power, and of love, and of a sound mind." (2 Timothy1:7)

CHAPTER 8

How to Cope with Adversity

To provide an amicable response to the two
basic questions relative to adversity

1. Why do bad things tend to happen to good people?
2. Why do good things tend to happen to bad people?

The universal outcry seems to be" Why"? Because God is omniscient, omnipotent, and omni loving, and omnipresent, why does God seemingly intervene with some situations and other situations He chooses not to intervene? As Debbie Ford wrote in her book that sometimes we do not obtain or ascertain answers because we have not asked the right question. I trust that right question begins with" Why floods, earthquakes, and wars?" These three kinds of disasters have been written in scriptures. The critical point is trials are referred to as a "refiner's fire." Can the Lord intervene? Absolutely, yes. Will He intervene in every adverse case and situation? No.

I don't want to infer that I have the solutions or answers to all the problems that occur in the world. What I can do is share some scriptures and thoughts from faithful leaders and theologians, a preponderate number of answers are possible for consideration. I have to try to adhere to the admonition of Isaiah: "Come now and let us reason together".

We must differentiate the words can and should. The scriptures state succinctly, "all things are possible with God, for He is all powerful." There should be no question as to whether God can prevent tragedies. Thus, the question turns on "Should He have intervened?" However, we make it too simple to say in the hour of misfortune "Couldn't God have prevented this?" The answer is obviously, yes. The center of the tragedy is the question, "why didn't He"? To ascertain the "right" answer you have to broach the right question. The right question is: What can I learn from this phenomenon? What meaning can I ponder at this unfortunate situation? What is the meaning of this? Sometimes bad things happen to really good people. It is part of life.

Faith vs Fear

Is the act a choice of faith or is it an act of fear? Hopefully, the decision and choice made reference to the question is couched in faith. Faith and fear are a semantic differential that are opposite to each other. They are mutually exclusive; if you choose faith then you don't submit to fear. Conversely, if you act with fear you lack faith. Consider an example of Jesus. Jesus was on the Sea of Galilee with the Apostles. "And He was in the ship…and there arose a great storm of wind, and the waves beat into the ship, that it was now full."

The apostles said unto him, "Master, carest thou not that we perish? And He arose and rebuked the wind, and He said unto the sea peace be still, and the wind ceased, and there was a great calm. And he said unto them, why are ye so fearful? How is it that ye have no faith? And the wind ceased and there was a great calm."

Why Jesus didn't intervene is a test that we must exercise faith. Consider a medical doctor who prescribes a certain drug to treat a symptom of PD for you. Both you and the doctor must exercise faith and have hope that the prescription will work. If the prescription doesn't work, you try something else. Is that false hope? It's not false hope because you still have faith and hope that the doctor will discover a drug to treat the cause of the problem and not merely treat the symptom. You faithfully trust the medical industry and have faith that someday the cause of PD will be discovered. Thus faith and work are not just reserved for the religious element of our society. Faith and work are the essence of discovery research. When someone commented to Emerson that he had failed at least a thousand times to discover the light bulb, his response was that he learned a thousand ways how to not create a light bulb.

Faith and hope generate confidence to accomplish whatever the mind can conceive and believe it can achieve. I call it the Columbus Approach. Columbus had faith and self-confidence integrated with the hope that he would succeed and accomplish his goal. Faith and hope empower individuals to have unbounded rationality and freedom of thought. Moreover, faith is the basis on which innovation and creativity are developed. Fear is the antithesis of faith. Fear of failure is perhaps the most self-destructive thinking possible. "As a man thinketh, so is he." For example, integratintg music therapy is frequently not attempted because of self-doubt and fear of what other people may think. Faith is the basis on which music therapy is based. The fourth leg of the three- legged stool complements the other three dimensions, physical, social, and mental. On the other hand, cynicism and skepticsism are the antithesis of faith. Faith empowers you to learn from the past, plan for the future, and live in the present. "They that do not learn from history are doomed to repeat it". As Jorge Santana stated, "Moreover, fear imposes artificial constraints on what is feasible and shuts down creativity. Faith is an opening to new thinking." To Quote President Roosevelt, (FDR) "The only thing we have to fear is fear itself." James, the apostle, said: "faith without works is dead." Keep the faith with good works.

Peter provides his insight and wisdom as he is familiar with the "fiery trial." "Beloved, think not it strange concerning the fiery trial which is to try as though some strange thing happened unto you."(Peter 4:12). Paul assures us that :"There hath no temptation taken you but such as is common to man: but God is faithful who will not suffer you to be tempted above that ye are able ; but will with the temptation also make a way to escape" (I Corinthians 10:13).

Job's patience is the classic example of coping with adversity. Even while his friends turned against him and accused him of committing sin, he remained faithful to the Lord. Moreover, the entire story of Job clearly indicated how he was blessed for his remaining faithful during the hardships. Thus, the punitive theory is false. Nevertheless the victim game turns on and the question lingers? "What have I done to deserve this? Our suffering is a form of a refiner's fire and the furnace of affliction, purging us of our sins as we hold fast to the Gospel of Jesus Christ.

Various Theories in Coping with Adversity

1.   The Illusory Theory

This theory suggests that evil is an illusion. Evil is a figment of our imagination. It is a the phantom of our minds. It is not real. It's all in your mind if you are suffering from a disease. The legitimate suffering is all in your mind. Reasoning follows this pattern. God is perfect, His creation is perfect. The world is perfect. You are a victim and can't see and know that this world is perfect. Therefore God is perfect and everything he created including mankind is perfect. Isaiah said some call evil good and good evil. Sometimes people cause their own instrument of misery by making imprudent decisions.

2.   The Privative Theory

God is a person; the challenge is to gain God's perspective. If you have the proper perspective, Venus de Milo is beautiful even without her arm. The underlying notion is that evil is not a positive reality but it is the absence of good. Satan is a privative being; he just isn't as good. This theory is really troubling. I saw wounded service men and women experiencing real pain; it would be real mockery to say to them: you really aren't experiencing pain. Evil does have a force in the world.

3.   The Instrumental Theory

Evil, love and suffering, opposition in the world are seen with an eternal perspective. They will not be destroyed. They are instruments of good outcomes. Thus, these instruments shape our lives. In Hebrews, "He was the son, yet learned he obedience by things which he suffered being made perfect. Be ye therefore perfect even as my Father in Heaven." Imperfection and suffering involve the work of perfection. "Precept on precept, here a little there a little."

4. Viktor Frankl's Logotherapy

During World War II, Viktor Frankl was incarcerated in Nazi death camps and endured several years of unspeakable horror. To find ways of healing sickness of the mind and of the spirit, he developed Logotherapy. Instead of asking, why me? He was asking why live? Why is life meaningful and purposeful? One of his famous quotes is:

"He who has a why to live for can bear almost any how." In his book, he explained that the core of his theory is the belief that man's primary motivational force is the search for meaning. The incredible attempts to dehumanize man at the concentration camps led Frankl to humanize man through logotherapy. He kept copious notes from which he developed his theory of logotherapy. Frankl is a professional writer who surpassed the rare ability to write in a layman's language level. As a longtime prisoner in bestial concentration camps, he wrote about the meaning and purpose of his existence. His father, mother, and brother died in those death camps. With the exception of his sister, his entire family perished in the camps. How could he survive, having every possession taken and suffering from hunger? How could he find life worth preserving? Moreover, his central theme of existentialism is to suffer, to survive and to find meaning in suffering. If there is a purpose in life at all, there must be a purpose in suffering and in dying. But no person can tell another what this purpose is. Each person must find out for himself and must accept the responsibility that his harasser prescribes.

One cannot but compare Frankl with Sigmund Freud. Both are physicians concerned with finding a cure for neurosis. Freud believes this distressing disorder is caused by the anxiety of conflicting unconscious motives. On the other hand, Frankl difference several forms of neurosis and links noogenic neurosis to the failure of the sufferer to find meaning and a sense of responsibility in his existence. Freud emphasized his frustration in the sexual person's life while Frankl stressed frustration in the will to discover meaning in all of life's vicissitudes.

5. Stockist Theory

Various forms of suffering are necessary in order to learn and teach the meaning for each unpleasant activity. It is necessary to experience the bad in order to appreciate the good things. Seeking the good helps people to keep themselves from the evil things in the world.

6. Loyalty of Job

He broaches the fundamental poignant question: "If a man dies shall he live again?"(Job 4:14) He answers his own question with an unequivocal, YES! (Job 14:14) After which reinforced his testimony of the reality of Jesus Christ: "For I know that my redeemer liveth and that he shall stand upon the earth in the latter day. And though after my skin worms destroy this body, yet in my flesh shall I see God." (Job 19:25,)
Can we trust God when confronted with life's trials? When we fail to see a real reason for suffering, does the suffering buttress our conviction and faith in Jesus Christ? The Biblical account of Job's hardships are indeed similar to trials to which we encounter today--namely financial ruin, bankruptcies, broken marriages, losses of assets, betrayal by closest friends, and the seemingly silence of God?"Job reframed the question, Why not me? He never lost his trust in God. Remember our slogan on our coins. In God we trust, everyone else must show identification.

7. C. S. Lewis Analogy

His explanation is that a remodeled house is quite different from the original house. Similarly the remodeled person is quite different from the original person especially if the remodeling was Christ centered. Thus if we endure some remodeling that could result in some suffering, we will prosper while on earth and following death and the resurrection, we can live with Jesus in his palace, His way. (Mere Christianity Ep.174).

8. Three Types of trials by Neil Maxwell

Type #1 Persecution from other religions

Brigham Young stated: "As to trials, bless your hearts, the man or woman who enjoys the spirit of our religion has no trials; but the man or woman who tries to live according to the Gospel of the Son of God, and at the same time, clings to the spirit of the world, has trials and sorrows, continually. Brigham Young Journal of Discourses (16:23)

Type # 2. Part of Living by Neil Maxwell

We came to earth by choice not by chance. John in the book of Revelations writes about the war in heaven during the Grand Council in which one third rejected the plan of God the Father and His Son. Salvation is grounded on agency or freedom to choose. We knew that there would be floods, earthquake, and murders. All the evil spirits on earth followed Satan the Son of the Morning. Accordingly, Satan and his angels are on earth raising HELL. Thus, the war in Heaven between good and evil is still present on earth. But the righteous will prevail because they are obedient to God's Law and through and by the Atonement of Jesus Christ the righteous will be saved. Matthew 5:45

The righteous will be united with the God the Father and the Son. Nevertheless, it takes a significant amount of faith to witness an automobile accident where the righteous dies physically but not spiritually, and the culprit responsible for the accident was intoxicated and was not injured in any way. As a medic in Vietnam, I saw some righteous soldiers die and some of the not so righteous live. The Gospel of Jesus Christ is not insurance against pain, it is a plan to enable you to endure the pain and progress.

#3 Neil Maxwell, Special Calling and Assignment

One other dimension of suffering occurs when the Omniscient Lord deliberately chooses you for some additional "hands on" training and education. Even though you are doing your best to live the two great commandments, the Apostle Paul informs us of the need for chastening. While speaking directly to the Hebrews: "For whom the Lord loveth he chastened and scourged every son whom He received. (Hebrew 12:6) The third reason for suffering is best illustrated by Paul indicating again to the Hebrews about Jesus "Though He was the Son yet learned He obedience by the things which he suffered, and being made perfect became the author of our salvation." (Hebrews 5:8) Remember the quote by Dr. Cartfired Broderick:

The Gospel of Jesus Christ is not insurance against pain. It is a resource in the event of pain. Terrible events can cause pain to good people. Job in the Bible is the epitome of this phenomenon.

9.　Spencer W. Kimball

"We knew before we were born that we were coming to earth for bodies and experience that we would have joys and sorrows, ease and pain, comforts and hardships, health and sickness, success and disappointments. We knew also that after a period of life we would die. We accepted these eventualities with gladness, eager to accept both the favorable and unfavorable. We eagerly accepted the chance to come to earth, even though it might be for only a day or a year. Perhaps we were not so much concerned whether we should die of disease or of senility. We were willing to take life as it came

"The Gospel teaches us there is no tragedy in death but the only tragedy is in sin."

10. Apostle Paul

"There hath no temptation taken you but such as is common to man: but God is faithful, who will not suffer you to be tempted above that ye are able; but will with the temptation also make a way to escape, that ye may be able to bear it." (1 Corinthians 10:13)

11. The faith of Shadrach, Meshach, and Abednego

These three Hebrews did not know if God would protect them from death. They responded by stating: "If it be so, our God whom we serve is able to deliver us from the burning fiery furnace, and He will deliver us out of thine hand, O King. But if not, be it known unto thee, O King, that we will not serve thy God's, nor worship the golden image which thou hast set-up." (Daniel 3:17)

The phrase, "but if not" constitutes an unconditional commitment. They were willing and able to take the heat because of their faith in God. There was a fourth in that fiery furnace with the valiant threesome, "and the form of the fourth is like the Son of God." (Daniel 3:25)

12. Joseph Smith's Experience in Carthage Jail, Illinois

When Joseph Smith was going to Carthage jail in Illinois, he made the following statement: "I am going like a lamb to the slaughter; but I am calm as a summer's morning; I have a conscience void of offense towards God and towards all men. I shall die innocent, and it shall yet be said of me- he was murdered in cold blood." Joseph Smith's Experience in the Liberty Jail

He wrote a long letter or a Psalm to the members. Following are a few excerpts from the letter to the members.

Question: "O God where art thou?"
Response: "Peace be unto thy soul."

Question: "How long will thy hand be stayed?"
Response : "If thou endure it well, God shall exalt thee on high; and thou shall triumph over all thy foes."

Response : "Thou art not yet as Job."
"Thy friends do not charge thee with the transgression, as they did Job."

Question: What power shall stay the heavens? How long can rolling waters remain impure?

Response: As well might men stretch forth his punny arm to stop the Missouri river in its decreed course or to turn it upstream, as to hinder the Almighty from pouring down knowledge from Heaven upon the heads of Latter-Day Saints.

"Jesus Descended below them all. Art thou greater than He?"

Joseph Smith's experience in the Richmond, Missouri jail. The following event was recorded in the autobiography of Parley P. Pratt, who was incarcerated with Joseph Smith.

"In one of those tedious nights …had listened for hours to the obscene and filthy language of our guards.….They even boasted of defiling by force wives and daughters, I knew he (Joseph Smith) was awake. On a sudden he arose to his feet, and spoke in a voice of thunder, or as the roaring lion, uttering the following words: Silence ye fiends of the infernal pit. In the name of Jesus Christ I rebuke you and command you to be still. I will not live another minute and bear such language. Cease such talk, or you or I die this instant". The guards lowered their weapons and dropped to their knees and begged his pardon.

Scripture

"There is no fear in love; but perfect love casteth out fear; because fear hath torment. He that feareth is not made perfect in love. (I John 4;18)

CHAPTER 9

How to Cope With
Compulsive Buyer Behavior

With a small percentage of PD patients, side effects from the medication has caused the patients to develop an insatiable impulse related to gambling, hypersexual, shopping, and eating disorders. Impulsive behavior is not congruent with a person's personality. Frequently impulsive behaviors manifest when new medications are added. The prescription list of the dosage of medication is increased significantly. If you notice such behaviors, it is important to tell your doctor as soon as possible. When the problem is not reported to the doctor, devastating results occur for some. The consequences have been divorce, catastrophes, debt, sexually transmitted diseases and overeating. The goal is to watch for these kinds of abnormal behaviors, before they get out of control and destroy people.

Propensity to Spend Money vs Propensity to Save Money

Individuals who are heavy in debt will most likely experience, the "triple threats"--depression, anxiety and stress. These are very prevalent with PD patients. The most common factors for divorce in the United States is failing to have a monthly operating budget and the inability of couples to obtain an amicable solution and money manage issues occur. There is the propensity to buy clothes, jewelry, cars, boats, and expensive guitars, to buy things they don't need, with money they don't have, to impress people they don't really like. This is the epitome of effective advertising.

The difference between an economic depression and a recession is a recession means your neighbor is unemployed and a depression means you are unemployed. You have to really fight emotional depression. One of the main issues with consumer buying is the impact on cash flow. When your outflow (expenses are greater than your inflow income) then you have negative cash flow. Most people tend to obtain another credit card. The net effect is that you are robbing Peter to pay Paul. You buy a tractor without a steering wheel and without a seat. His response is "well you have lost your butt and you don't know which way to turn."

Cash Flow, Cash Flow, Cash Flow

To prepare a cash flow statement, follow these steps:

Step 1. Add all disposable income, earnings after taxes, (EAT).

Step 2. Add all fixed and variable costs. Rent or a mortgage payment is a fixed cost; eating out at McDonald's is a variable cost.

Step 3. Subtract total costs from total revenues, if total costs are greater than total revenue you are in the canal drinking canal water. It is called a negative cash flow. Two alternatives are available:

1. Do nothing

Have creditors calling you names that you can't find in Webster's College Dictionary 2nd edition. You respond by claiming that your financial problems are a result of PD. You try to borrow from friends and family and they tell you H---- NO three times, tell you to take a hike to Mt. Ogden and cool off and be reasonable. You believe that Thomas Hobbes was right, "The life of man is solitary, poor, nasty, brutish, and short."

2. Take corrective action

With a prompt and reasonable start and with all deliberate speed to take control of your finances, sit down with your significant other or your spouse and answer this poignant question: "Will a man rob God? But ye say wherein have we robbed thee? In tithes and offerings. Ye are cursed with a curse, even this whole nation. Bring ye all the tithes into the storehouse that there may be meat in mine house, and prove me now herewith, saith the Lord of host, if I will not open you the windows of heaven and pour you out a blessing that there shall not room to receive it and I will rebuke the devourer for your sakes and he shall not destroy the fruits of your ground."(Malachi 3:8-11).

Now you're thinking how can I pay tithing, which is 10% of my total income, before tax deductions, with a negative cash flow? Answer, if you pay 10% on your gross salary or wages, the Lord will open up the windows of heaven. If you don't have a job, the Lord will help you find one. Tithing is predicated on faith. Prove him herewith. I can attest that tithing is a real blessing. I have been unemployed with five kids just before Christmas. I paid tithing on whatever pitance I could earn and in January after Christmas, I found a full time job. Tithing works. It is the best unemployment insurance available. While I was a missionary for the Church of Jesus Christ of Latter-day Saints in Brazil, I taught many Brazilians who were unemployed. I had them read the promise of the Lord through Malachi. Some joined the LDS Church and started paying tithing and found purposeful employment. Some may claim that tithing is similar to a regressive flat tax. The affluent get off easy only paying 10% of huge income, whereas, the poor also pay 10% of a small income. It is a big bite out of a small pie, and for the affluent, a small bite from a large pie. For this reason, Congress has passed a progressive tax which means the more an individual makes, the more tax they pay, based on the ability to pay.

The Widow's Mite

The Lord requires tithing across the board regardless of income, then that is good enough for me! Study Malachi, the affluent do not receive a larger portion of blessings. The same windows of heaven are open to everybody who lives the law of tithing faithfully, regardless of the amount The story of the widow's mite illustrates the concept quite nicely story in the Gospel of Luke in the New Testament; the story of the poor widow and her two mites and which merit analysis; it cannot be ignored. "And he (Jesus) looked up, and saw the rich men casting their gifts into the treasure. And he saw also a certain poor widow casting in thither two mites. And he said, of a truth I say unto you, that this poor widow hath cast in more than they all: For all these have of their abundance cast in unto the offerings of God; but she of her penury hath cast in all the living that she had."(Luke 21:1-4) Gifts to the Lord are not measured by the monetary amount offered but by what it is in their heart, and not what is left over after the gift is given. The widow gave two mites because it was unacceptable to give only one mite. One mite was considered too small an amount even for the lowest Jew. Jesus neither rejected the gifts given to him nor did He belittle or ridicule the rich men who gave their abundance. The widow's gift was acceptable because of the sacrifice the widow made. Jesus placed sacrifice on a higher level by making it a dimension of giving.

In Mere Christianity, C.S. Lewis proffers some sage advice with his usual practicality: "I do not believe one can settle how much we ought to give. I am afraid the only safe rule is to give more than we can spare. In other words, if your expenses on comforts, luxuries, and other amusements, etc. is up to the standard common among those with the same income as our own, we are probably giving away too little. If our charities do not at all pinch or hamper us, I should say they are too small. There ought to be things we should like to do and cannot do because our charitable expenditures exclude them."

Cash flow Analysis

If your outflow is less than your inflow, then you have some leftover money to spend prudently, according to your own amicable distribution of the money. The Rule Of Thumb is that you should pay yourself or save at least 10% of your discretionary money for an emergency precaution if a disaster strikes, or unfortunate event occurs. On the other hand, if your outflow is greater than your inflow then you would have A NEGATIVE CASHFLOW, whereby your upkeep will lead to your to your downfall.

If no corrective action is implemented, bankruptcy is frequently the alternative selected. Remove yourself from the Canal Zone expediously, stop drinking canal water, and decrease spending. Remember Lee's Maxim: don't buy things you don't need with money you don't have and don't try to impress people you really don't like.

Wants vs Needs

Wants are not the same as needs. A need must be periodically satisfied in order to live; Abraham Maslow hierarchy of needs indicates that shelter and safety are the basic needs for survival. A want is on a wish list. You need a car to drive to work but do you need a Ferrari or Porsche? If you are in a negative cash flow, then needs take priority and presence.

Opportunity Costs

If you buy a Ferrari, then you cannot use the same money to buy a 23- foot wakeboarding boat. Limited funds pose a financial constraint and preclude buying both items. You have to choose among alternative items to which you need presently. With opportunity cost is an inherent giving up or trading off one item for the other item. Thus, if you buy the boat you are constrained in buying a car. And vice versa, if you buy the car, you are unable to buy the boat. Some people will attempt to buy both on credit, thereby creating a huge debt with high interest rates. Debt enslaves you. The principle of compound interest applies to loans with an unpaid balance. Interest increases on unpaid debt. You can work either for money or money can work for you. You are free to choose. Choose wisely. Depression, anxiety, and stress are the predictable symptoms of poor personal financial management and these problems are exacerbated by PD. The sunken costs typically incurred by a herculean debt tend to be a key factor in almost all divorces.

"Pay Thy Debt and Live"

Ponder and reflect on the following quotes:

1. "Think what you do when you run in debt; you give over to another power over you liberty." Benjamin Franklin.
2. "I have discovered the philosopher's stone that turns everything into gold: it is pay as you go. John Randolph.
3. "Do not accustom yourself to consider debt only as an inconvenience; you will find it a calamity." Samuel Johnson.
4. "Poverty is hard, but debt is horrible." Charles Haddon Spurgeon.
5. "The debt-habit is the twin brother poverty." Theodore Thornton Munger.

Summary

1. Love of money is the root of all evil.
2. Treasures on earth vs. treasures in Heaven.
3. What doth it profits a man to gain the whole world and lose his soul? What can a man give in exchange for his soul?
4. Financial Do's and Don'ts

Do's:

* Ensure that both spouses are jointly setting financial goals.
* Create a retirement fund comprised of no-load mutual funds, 401 K or IRA's
* Pray for inspiration before desperation hits you.
* Share your financial resources with others when possible.
* Pay tithing and other offerings generously.
* Investigate a company prior to investing.
* Determine your tolerance for risk prior to investing.
* Assess if you are a risk taker or a risk averter.

Remember there are more pyramids in Utah than in Egypt.

*   Invest wisely.

Realize if you lose money you will not miss it.

<u>Don'ts:</u>

*   Abdicate responsibility for financial management to one
*   Engage in conspicuous consumption in which you need Big toys.
*   Borrow money either from friends or family.
*   Lend money either to friends, or to family members
*   Make a major purchase when you are: hungry, angry, lonely, or tired (HALT)

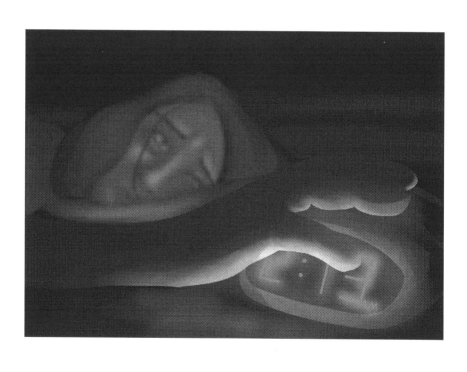

C H A P T E R   1 0

How to Cope With Sleeping Problems

Commonly Overlooked PD Condition

Approximately 80% of Parkinson's Disease patients have sleep problems. Yet sleep disorders remain under reported by patients and under diagnosed by a few physicians. Sleep dysfunctions have a negative impact on the lives of patients and caregivers. Poor sleep frequently worsens the PD symptoms and increases the risk of depression and anxiety. Recent research discovered that poor nocturnal sleep and longstanding daytime sleepiness may be risk factors for PD. The fact is PD patients are confronted with a few unique barriers to obtaining sufficient sleep. The barrier tends to be unpleasant side effects from medications. Often prescribed medications may interact and cause illness. Such was the case with my mother who suffered among other things PD. Several incidents occurred in which she suffered nausea that was attributed to drugs that were contraindicated.

Sleep Hygiene for a Better Sleep

Following are a few suggestions to enhance a better sleep:

1. Wake up at the same time every day.

This will create a circadian rhythm, whereby you wake up at the same time daily using an alarm.

2. Limit day time naps to one per day.

Only one nap for a maximum of 45 minutes should not adversely affect falling asleep in the evening.

3. Use caution when taking cold medicines.

Some headache medicines contain stimulants that can impede a restful sleep

4. Exercise regularly in the morning.

Review Chapter 4 of this book which discusses the significance of sleep habits.

5. Establish a sleep ritual.

Every night brush your teeth, read, and plan the next day.

6. Read and listen to soft music before getting into bed.

Review Chapter 5 in this book that deals with anxiety.

7. Worry before getting in bed.

Offer a prayer alone and also with your family.

8. Keep your bedroom fairly dark.

Night lights are essential to minimize the risk of falling.

A somewhat cool temperature is normally far more comfortable than a hot stuffy room temperature. However, comfortable temperature is very subjective. Play a little classical music.

9. Block out ambient noise.

Designate certain hours during the course of day as quiet hours. Establish curfew hours for the evenings.

Refer to Chapter 7.

Obviously you cannot find lost time. Also, it is one resource with which we are all equal. Study the time management grid in Chapter 7. You make time to do the activities you enjoy.

Following are sample questions from the Parkinson's Disease Sleep Scale:

1. Do you experience numbness or tingling of your armor legs?
2. Do you have painful muscle cramps?
3. Do you unexpectedly fall asleep during the day?
4. Do you experience tremors?

IF YOU ANSWERED YES TO ANY OF THE AFOREMENTIONED QUESTIONS, CONTACT A NEUROLOGIST. (1-800-4PD-INFO)

With PD patients, the most prevalent sleep disorders are analyzed below:

1. Insomnia

The individual wakes up during the night and has trouble going back to sleep again. It usually falls into two categories: If you can't fall asleep initially, it is called Sleep One. If you fall asleep wake up several times, about every two hours, it is called Maintenance Insomnia.

2. Rapid eye movement REM and RBD

During the Rapid Movement. (RBM) The individuals act out their dreams by talking, or shouting. During the Rapid Behavior Disorder

(RBD) phase of sleep, hitting or punching could occur, thereby endangering the eye.

3. Sleep Apnea

Breathing is interrupted while the person is sleeping because the throat is blocked momentarily by the tongue or other tissues. As a result, excessive daytime sleepiness occurs because of numerous brief awakenings during the night.

The following are the symptoms of Sleep Apnea:

- Headaches
- Blurred vision
- Weakness in arms and legs
- Difficulty speaking
- Dizziness

Treatment:

- * Do not to sleep on your back.
- * See a physical therapist.
- * Apply neurologic music therapy.

4. Daytime Sleepiness

This condition could cause a "sleep attack" in which a sudden onset of sleep occurs without warning and may lead to a serious accident.

5. Restless Leg Syndrome (RLS)

This is a symptom of PD of which I can personally testify can be very annoying. For example, you could be giving a speech or a presentation and your legs decide to try and take a walk. As to symptoms, normally you will feel a tingling or creeping sensation just prior to your legs mounting an assault, according to Lisa Fields, who is a New Jersey based freelancer.

Research of PD Problems

The Parkinson's Disease and Movement Disorders Center at North Western University in Chicago, has developed a unique clinic dedicated to the early diagnosis and comprehensive treatment of a wide variety of sleep problems related to PD and other neurological disorders. The research approach undertaken at this Center is based on collaboration. The research brings together specialists in sleep medicine with the goal of developing new therapies for PD and sleep disorders associated with PD. The National Parkinson Foundation is working with the North Western with the Disease and Movement Center at Northwestern University to support sleep research and bring the issue to the forefront.

Empirical recent research has shown that classical music improves the lives of people with PD who listen to peaceful music prior to retiring for the night. Music therapy should as well help people with other sleeping issues. Thus, sleep therapies integrated with Classical Music should also improve the lives of people with PD and concurrently and improve those with sleeping disorders.

According to the National Sleep Foundation, 47% of the people who were identified as being sleep deprived, admitted to being significantly more impatient and sarcastic with customers and work associates. Therefore, sufficient sleep or lack thereof can affect an individual's mood, and thereby impact family and social relations.

Waking up refreshed will not only affect the individuals' mood, but also their attitude. Dr. Brendan Lucey, Director of the Sleep Medicine Center at Washington University School of Medicine, noted that 40% of workers surveyed randomly in an assembly setting, suffered from sleep deprivation. Dr. Michael Breus, Director of The American Academy of Sleep Medicine said: "The better rested the workers are, the better they are going to perform and give customers what they there looking for."

Conclusion

Enjoy the abundant life which is comprised of the following:

1. Be an optimist. "Things turn out best for those who make the best of the way things turn out."
2. Focus on the positives even in challenging situations.
3. Differentiate an optimist from a pessimist i s the way they describe good and bad events.
4. Use self-talk or auto suggestion.
5. Practice Self-talk to make an impression on your mind.
6. Develop a positive mental attitude.
7. Guard against negative self-talk.
8. Work to imprint positive talk on the subconscious mind.
9. Be an active and reflective listener.
10. Don't interrupt another person who is talking.
11. Laugh often.
12. Stay motivated.
13. Accomplish your goals with all deliberate speed.
14. Reframe a problem by breaking it down into smaller parts.

Concluding Thoughts

The four dimensions of life include the following:

1. Physical:

* Exercise daily.
* Find an activity that generates endorphins.

2. Spiritual:

* Seek inspiration from the Almighty who giveth understanding.
* Believe in prayer and that it is good medicine.
* Study the scriptures daily.
* Enjoy classical music.

3. Mental:

* Be a lifelong-learner.
* Realize that cognition is vital for PD patients.
* Learn a foreign language.
* Buy an inexpensive guitar and start learning.
* Keep your mind alert by mental exercise.

4. Social:

* Help a neighbor to learn how to play a musical instrument.
* Discover a purposeful life is predicated n service.
* Remember service is not spelled "serve us."
* Service of others will normally produce reciprocity.

The trick is to keep these four dimensions in balance.

Daily Scripture

"Have I not commanded you? Be strong and of a good courage; Be strong and of a good courage; be not afraid, neither be thou dismayed: for the Lord thy God is with thee whithersoever thou goest." (Joshua 1:9)

References:

Alfred Publishing Co., *Essential Dictionary of Music* (1978) Van Nuys, CA

Consumer Reports (1950) The *Midlife Show,* NY, NY

Copeland, Aaron (1988) What *To Look for In Music*, NY, NY

Randolph, David (1989) *This Is Music*, Chicago, IL

James, William, (1902) The Varieties of Religious Experience, Mentor Book, CA

Siegel, Bernie Sharper Collins Publishing (Inc.1993). New York, New York

Copeland, Aaron, (1999) What *To Listen for In Music Inc.*, USA: McGraw-Hill, Inc.

Randolph, David, (1964) *This Is Music, New York, New York*: McGraw-Hill, Inc.

James, William, (1960) The *Varieties of Religious Experience*

Hinckley, K.C., (1989) *A compact Guide to the Christian Life*: Wheaton, Ilinois: Navpress Books

Greenwood, Lee, (2001) *God Bless the USA*, Nashville, Tennessee Rutledge Hill Press

Ives, Burl, (1953) *Burl Ives Song Book,* New York, New York: Ballantine Books, Inc.

Rosen, Diana, (2001) *American Pride, New York*, New York: Citadel Press

Wolford, Darwin, (1995) Song *of the Righteous*, Springville, Utah: Cedar Fort Inc.

Seeger, Pete, (1960) American *Favorite Ballads, New* York, New York: Oak Publication

National Board of Young Men's Christian Association, (1968) *Folk Songs and Hymns with Guitar Accompaniment*, New York, New York: USA

Wier, Albert E. (1915) *Piano Pieces the Whole World Plays,* New York, NY: D. Appleton and Company

Simon, Henry W. (1945) *A treasury of Grand Opera,* New York, New York: Simon and Schuster, Inc.

Book, Elaine. (2015) *Reframe thinking, Rutgers*, State University. National Parkinson's Disease Foundation

Dobkin, Roseanne D. (2017) *What is Parkinson's Disease?* Parkinson's Disease Foundation

Fox, Michael J. (2014) *Smell is often Overlooked as a PD non-motor Symptom* Michael J. Fox Parkinson's Disease Foundation

Lewis, C.S. (1890*) Mere Christianity*, Harper San Francisco,

Dossey, Larry. (1996) *Prayer is Good Medicine*, Harper San Francisco

Gelb, Michael. (1998) *How to Think Like Leonardo da Vinci*. New York, NY Dela Conte Press.

Murray, Andrew. (2002) *31-Day Guide to Prayer*, Barbour Publishing, Inc.

Banks, Joseph and Borrowman, Jerry. (2006) *A Distant Prayer*, Covenant Coma Inc.

Poelman, Catherine E. (2002) *How to Make a Difference*, Shadow Mountain, Salt Lake City, Utah

Printed in the United States
By Bookmasters